Forgiveness: Not Necessarily What You Think

Forgiveness: Not Necessarily What You Think

What the Bible Really Says, and What it Doesn't Say

Sister Renee Pittelli

Scripture quotations identified KJV are taken from the King James Version of the Bible.

Pertaining to Scripture quotations identified NKJV:
Scripture taken from the New King James Version. Copyright 1979, 1980, 1982 by Thomas Nelson, Inc. Used by permission. All rights reserved.

Pertaining to Scripture quotations identified NIV:
Scripture taken from the HOLY BIBLE, NEW INTERNATIONAL VERSION. Copyright 1973, 1978, 1984 by International Bible Society. Used by permission of Zondervan. All rights reserved.

Pertaining to Scripture quotations identified NASB:
"Scripture taken from the NEW AMERICAN STANDARD BIBLE, Copyright 1960, 1962, 1963, 1968, 1971, 1972, 1973, 1975, 1977, 1995 by The Lockman Foundation. Used by permission."

Pertaining to Scripture quotations identified NLT:
Scripture quotations are taken from the Holy Bible, New Living Translation, copyright 1996. Used by permission of Tyndale House Publishers, Inc., Wheaton, IL 60189. All rights reserved.

ISBN-13: 9781979182126
ISBN-10: 1979182124

Dedicated to the Truth-Seekers

AND YE SHALL KNOW THE TRUTH, AND THE TRUTH SHALL MAKE YOU FREE....John 8:32 KJV

Table Of Contents

Introduction

Forgiveness: Not Necessarily What You Think

TAKE HEED TO YOURSELVES: IF THY BROTHER TRESPASS AGAINST THEE, REBUKE HIM; AND IF HE REPENT, FORGIVE HIM......Luke 17:3 KJV.

AND WHEN YE STAND PRAYING, FORGIVE, IF YE HAVE OUGHT AGAINST ANY: THAT YOUR FATHER ALSO WHICH IS IN HEAVEN MAY FORGIVE YOU YOUR TRESPASSES. BUT IF YE DO NOT FORGIVE, NEITHER WILL YOUR FATHER WHICH IS IN HEAVEN FORGIVE YOUR TRESPASSES.....Mark 11:25-26 KJV.

FORGIVE AS THE LORD FORGAVE YOU......Colossians 3:13 NIV.

Brothers and Sisters, our Father wants us to forgive. We all know this is not easy; in fact, it can be very difficult. The Enemy is jubilant when we do not forgive. But our hearts must be obedient to our beloved Father, first and foremost, above all else. We must overcome Satan's temptation to remain unforgiving.

However, forgiveness and the requirement to forgive are not necessarily what we have been led to believe by our abusers and their Flying Monkeys, or by others who are either misinformed or trying to deceive us. There are conditions for being forgiven. *God's formula for forgiveness is repentance* **first**, *and* **then** *forgiveness.*

Luke 17:3 is the scripture most often misquoted, usually by the abuser or his Flying Monkeys, when he tells you that the Bible says "Forgive and forget," or that you must forgive him because you are a Christian. However, Jesus is very specific when he tells us to *rebuke* the one who hurt us first, and to forgive him *only if he repents*. Have you rebuked your abuser, and has he or she repented?

The Bible tells us to forgive *as God forgave us* (Ephesians 4:32; Colossians 3:13).God forgives us when, and *only* when, we come to him, confess our sin, ask for forgiveness (apologize), and *repent* (turn from our sinful ways) (Ezekiel 33:10-20; Isaiah 55:6-7; Jeremiah 6:16-30; Jeremiah 26:3; Luke 13:3, 5; Acts 3:19). He does *not* forgive those who are "stiff-necked" and stubborn, refuse to repent, and continue to do evil- and he does not expect us to, either. The Lord does not expect more of us than he himself is willing to do! Do we imagine ourselves to be holier than God? God requires repentance, and so must we. By forgiving unre-morseful evildoers, we are depriving them of the opportunity to repent and transform their lives.

In Luke 17:3, Jesus tells us very clearly that we are to forgive someone who sins against us *if* he repents. In context, this verse refers to a "brother"-a fellow believer. Some take this to mean that the same repentance is not required of a non-believer who damages you, although I fail to see the logic in this. Why would Jesus *not* want repentance to be required of non-believers as well, knowing that remorse, humility, and changing their evil ways could only serve to bring their hearts closer to him? God does not want us to continue to be abused. Instead, the Lord tells us repeatedly to shun evildoers- whether they claim to be fellow believers or not- and have nothing further to do with them (Deuteronomy 19:19; Psalm 37:9; Psalm 101:3-8; Psalm 119:115; Psalm 129:1-4; Proverbs 22:10, 24-25; Proverbs 23:9; Proverbs 25: 4-5; Matthew 18:17; Titus 3:10-11; 1 Corinthians 5:1-5, 11). In the Bible, the children of God are repeatedly told not to contaminate ourselves by associating with the children of the devil.

God wants us to be open-hearted and *willing to forgive*, if and when our abuser repents and changes her ways. If there is true repentance, the Lord does want us to forgive. But he does not want us to cheapen forgiveness by giving it prematurely and undeservedly to those who have every intention of continuing on in their evil.

In this book, we are going to study the scriptures that talk about forgiveness and repentance, including relevant context and commentary, as well as dilemmas and questions we are often faced with. I have made every effort to thoroughly search out every relevant scripture. If you find any I missed, please make sure to read them in context, keeping in mind the fundamental premises about the Bible which we will discuss in Chapter 1. You may be surprised to learn that forgiveness and God's instructions to forgive are not necessarily what you have been led to believe they are.

May God bless you in your struggle to forgive those who have wronged you when they truly make amends and change their ways. With courage from the Lord, the devil and his tricks to separate us from God's grace, will be defeated. For our God is a mighty God! Hallelujah!

Chapter 1

Fundamental Truths About God's Word

All Bible study needs to be based on certain premises that should go without saying. First, let's clarify some facts about the Bible and the Lord. These address some of the things that the devil and his children will say to cause us to doubt ourselves and to cause confusion when we confront their evil. Remember that the devil is the author of confusion and the father of lies. It will help to keep these points in mind as you continue reading this book, and we will discuss many of them in more detail:

1. People who abuse other people are not children of God, no matter what they might claim. No real Christian can be an abuser, an abuse-enabler, or an abuse-defender. There is no such thing. Anyone who abuses or betrays you, deliberately puts you in a position of being abused by someone else, or pressures you to overlook, tolerate, or allow yourself to continue being abused, is not a child of God. He is a child of Satan. Keep this in mind as you read the rest of this book and when deciding how to deal with an abuser.
2. Children of Satan are not "good" people. They do not "have some good in them." God himself calls them "evil"

and "wicked." There is no gray area here. It is black and white in the Bible.

3. Remember that phony holier-than-thou "Christians" will insist that they are righteous and godly, but they are the spawn of Satan, and therefore liars (John 8:44). They are the wolves in sheep's clothing that Jesus warned us about (Matthew 7:15). You will be able to tell them by their fruits (Matthew 7:16), not by what they say, if you have an opportunity to observe them for a while. These are the things Jesus himself teaches us. Some people can quote plenty of Scripture, but still have absolutely no grasp of its true meaning. The Bible tells us not to believe every spirit, but to test the spirits and see if they are from God (1 John 4:1-6). Do not believe them when they judge you for standing up to evil. Real Christians are supposed to take a stand against evil. Anyone who tries to defend or facilitate evil is evil himself.

4. We are not supposed to "live in peace" with the children of Satan. That would be absurd. Biblical teachings to "live in peace" are addressed to God's children concerning the rest of the children of God. In His Word, the Lord repeatedly tells his children to stand up to evil, stay away from the devil's children and shun the wicked. This does not mean we don't "love" them, and it is not "taking revenge." It does not make us "unloving" or "vengeful." We can love them just fine from a safe distance, we are doing *nothing at all* to them by simply staying away, and we are being obedient to our Father. We are not to contaminate ourselves with the wicked. It is preposterous to teach that the Lord wants his children to live in peace with, or to even associate with, the children of Satan. See my book The Christian's Guide to No Contact for more information on this and relevant scriptures.

5. The Bible is written as instructions for godly people to get along with other godly people. *It is not written for the*

godly to get along with the ungodly. It is written for the children of God, not the children of the devil. Instructions to honor and obey are meant for *godly* parents. We are not supposed to obey the evil. We are not supposed to honor the wicked. It is preposterous for anyone to teach that God tells us to obey evil people or honor the wicked.

6. God never tells us to lie about others' bad behavior or to cover up evil. We are always instructed to expose evil and tell the truth. In fact, God commands us not to bear *false* witness against our neighbor. This can apply to good or bad behavior. It is preposterous for anyone to teach that God wants us to lie.

7. When a scripture uses the word "brother," it is specifically referring to a brother (or sister) in Christ, a fellow believer. Not a phony "Christian," but a genuine Christian. Almost every scripture about forgiveness refers specifically to forgiving fellow believers, not the children of the devil, and we have already established that abusers and backstabbers are not true fellow believers. God instructs us to be forgiving toward our brothers and sisters in Christ (who, by definition, will not have a problem with godly repentance) so there will not be divisions in the Body of Christ, and so the young church, just starting to be built at the time the gospels were written, could grow. When we read the one or two verses about forgiveness that do not specifically mention fellow believers, *this still does not mean that verse is referring to forgiving, and certainly not to reconciling with, the children of Satan.*

8. Keep in mind that if we are upset at a nice, normal, well-meaning person, who usually respects our boundaries and treats us well, and who inadvertently offended us, that is not the same thing as someone who abuses us repeatedly, behaves with malice or has committed a major betrayal against us, not caring that we would be hurt. In the normal

course of normal relationships, small hurts happen regularly, and we all forgive them and overlook them on a regular basis. *This is proof that we do have forgiving hearts and are willing to forgive,* which is what God wants. We should feel able to communicate our hurt or anger, and the person who truly didn't mean any harm should have no problem making amends and not doing it again (this is repentance). The Lord wants us to have a forgiving heart and be willing to forgive those we love and who truly love us. That is not the same thing as allowing abuse and evil to thrive unchallenged.

9. We are instructed to forgive those who have hurt us if and when they repent. *There is no example of unconditional forgiveness in the Bible.* Repentance is always required. Jesus himself specifies this in Luke 17:3. Repentance is not a mere apology, but a change in behavior. The reason it is so rare for us to be able to forgive our abusers is that the children of the devil almost never repent of their evil. This is neither our fault nor our responsibility, and there is nothing we can do about it. It is one-hundred percent on them.

10. True repentance includes godly remorse and sorrow, concerned only with the feelings and welfare of the victim, making it up to her or making her whole. Godly repentance also means never doing it again, turning from evil and becoming a new person in Christ. Ungodly remorse and ungodly sorrow, on the other hand, are only displayed to benefit the perpetrator in some way- to make his life easier, to get forgiven so things can "go back to normal," to stay out of jail, to avoid paying a debt, to make him look good to other people, etc. In this case, whatever "repentance" is shown is phony and unacceptable for forgiveness.

11. Forgiveness has nothing to do with reconciliation. If a child of Satan apologizes, it is usually because she wants

something. She expects to be back in our lives and for everything to go "back to normal." But there is no such biblical requirement. Forgiveness does not require exposing yourself again to someone who has damaged you in the past. We can forgive just fine and still keep our distance.

12. There is no deadline on forgiveness. We are not required to forgive on demand, or on the basis of a mere apology without evidence of godly repentance, which may take a significant amount of time to observe. We are also not required to announce our forgiveness to anyone. Forgiveness is between us and God, no one else.

The important points to remember from this chapter are:

* God calls people who abuse or betray other people "wicked," "evil", and "children of the devil." God instructs his children to have nothing to do with Satan's children.

* God wants us to have a forgiving heart and be willing to forgive when the wicked truly turn from their evil. He commands us to forgive if and when they repent of their evil ways. *The reason we are biblically unable to forgive is that the wicked refuse to repent.* Ungodly, self-serving "repentance" doesn't count.

* Just because someone claims to be a fellow believer, does not mean they really are. Most verses about forgiveness are concerned with avoiding divisions within the church and settling disagreements between the children of God, not with outsiders and certainly not with the wicked, who are lying about being a sister or brother in Christ.

Chapter 2

Things the Bible Says About the Requirement of Repentance Before Forgiveness

There are scriptures that talk about God's forgiveness, and then there are scriptures that talk about man's forgiveness. Many abusers and abuse-defenders like to insist that these are two separate issues in terms of the prerequisite of repentance. They preach that God's forgiveness is somehow "different" than man's forgiveness, in that God always requires repentance, but for some reason, man is not supposed to do the exact same thing and follow the model that God lays out for us. Of course, the rest of the time, they accuse us of *not* being "godly," but in this particular instance, it works in their favor to *tell us* not to be "godly."

What the wicked say about repentance not being necessary and forgiveness having to be granted on demand is, of course, not true. It is another lie of the devil. Jesus himself contradicts their assertion in Luke 17:3, which is specifically about man's forgiveness of another man:

> *TAKE HEED TO YOURSELVES: IF **THY BROTHER** TRES-PASS AGAINST THEE, REBUKE HIM; AND **IF HE REPENT**, FORGIVE HIM…Luke 17:3 KJV.*

*Context~ *THEN SAID HE UNTO THE DISCIPLES, IT IS IMPOSSIBLE BUT THAT OFFENCES WILL COME: BUT WOE UNTO HIM, THROUGH WHOM THEY COME! IT WERE BETTER FOR HIM THAT A MILLSTONE WERE HANGED ABOUT HIS NECK, AND HE CAST INTO THE SEA, THAN THAT HE SHOULD OFFEND ONE OF THESE LITTLE ONES. TAKE HEED TO YOURSELVES: IF THY BROTHER TRESPASS AGAINST THEE, REBUKE HIM; AND **IF HE REPENT**, FORGIVE HIM, AND IF HE TRESPASS AGAINST THEE SEVEN TIMES IN A DAY, **AND SEVEN TIMES IN A DAY TURN AGAIN TO THEE, SAYING, I REPENT**; THOU SHALT FORGIVE HIM...Luke 17:1-4 KJV.*

*Commentary~ Jesus is very clear that we are to rebuke an offender, and forgive him *if he repents*. Most Holier-Than-Thous who criticize us for not forgiving very conveniently overlook the entire middle part of this verse which talks about rebuking and repentance. It is almost unheard-of for an evil person to come to us even once and repent, much less seven times in a day. *Not because of our "un-forgiveness,"* but because of their own "stiff-necked," stubborn refusal to give up their wickedness, the forgiving-seven-times-in-a-day part of the scripture will pretty much never apply to our situations.

The following verses talk about God's forgiveness, and repentance being a condition of it. Note that God does not "forgive everyone." We are only forgiven if and when we repent of our sins:

*AND GOD SAW THEIR WORKS, THAT **THEY TURNED FROM THEIR EVIL WAY**; AND GOD REPENTED OF THE EVIL, THAT HE HAD SAID THAT HE WOULD DO UNTO THEM; AND HE DID IT NOT....Jonah 3:10 KJV.*

*BUT IF THE WICKED WILL **TURN FROM ALL HIS SINS THAT HE HATH COMMITTED, AND KEEP ALL MY STATUTES, AND DO THAT WHICH IS LAWFUL AND RIGHT**, HE SHALL SURELY LIVE, HE SHALL NOT DIE. ALL HIS TRANSGRESSIONS THAT HE HATH COMMITTED, THEY SHALL NOT BE MENTIONED UNTO HIM: IN HIS RIGHTEOUSNESS THAT HE HATH DONE HE SHALL LIVE. HAVE I ANY PLEASURE AT ALL THAT THE WICKED SHOULD DIE? SAITH THE LORD GOD: AND NOT THAT HE SHOULD RETURN FROM HIS WAYS, AND LIVE?... Ezekiel 18:21-23 KJV.*

*THEREFORE, I WILL JUDGE YOU, O HOUSE OF ISRAEL, EVERY ONE ACCORDING TO HIS WAYS, SAITH THE LORD GOD. **REPENT**, AND TURN YOURSELVES FROM ALL YOUR TRANSGRESSIONS; SO INIQUITY SHALL NOT BE YOUR RUIN. CAST AWAY FROM YOU ALL YOUR TRANSGRESSIONS, WHEREBY YE HAVE TRANSGRESSED; AND MAKE YOU A NEW HEART AND A NEW SPIRIT: FOR WHY WILL YE DIE, O HOUSE OF ISRAEL? FOR I HAVE NO PLEASURE IN THE DEATH OF HIM THAT DIETH, SAITH THE LORD GOD: WHEREFORE TURN YOURSELVES, AND LIVE YE…Ezekiel 18:30-32 KJV.*

SAY UNTO THEM, AS I LIVE, SAITH THE LORD GOD, I HAVE NO PLEASURE IN THE DEATH OF THE WICKED; BUT THAT THE WICKED TURN FROM HIS WAY AND LIVE; TURN YE, TURN YE FROM YOUR EVIL WAYS; FOR WHY WILL YE DIE, O HOUSE OF ISRAEL? THEREFORE, THOU SON OF MAN, SAY UNTO THE CHILDREN OF THY

PEOPLE, **THE RIGHTEOUSNESS OF THE RIGHTEOUS SHALL NOT DELIVER HIM IN THE DAY OF HIS TRANSGRESSION***; AS FOR THE WICKEDNESS OF THE WICKED, HE SHALL NOT FALL THEREBY IN THE DAY THAT HE TURNETH FROM HIS WICKEDNESS;* **NEITHER SHALL THE RIGHTEOUS BE ABLE TO LIVE FOR HIS RIGHTEOUSNESS IN THE DAY THAT HE SINNETH***. WHEN I SAY TO THE RIGHTEOUS, THAT HE SHALL SURELY LIVE; IF HE TRUST TO HIS OWN RIGHTEOUSNESS, AND COMMIT INIQUITY, ALL HIS RIGHTEOUSNESS SHALL NOT BE REMEMBERED; BUT FOR HIS INIQUITY THAT HE HATH COMMITTED, HE SHALL DIE FOR IT. AGAIN, WHEN I SAY TO THE WICKED, THOU SHALL SURELY DIE; IF HE TURN FROM HIS SIN AND DO THAT WHICH IS LAWFUL AND RIGHT;* **IF THE WICKED RESTORE THE PLEDGE, GIVE AGAIN THAT HE HAD ROBBED, WALK IN THE STATUTES OF LIFE, WITHOUT COMMITTING INIQUITY; HE SHALL SURELY LIVE***, HE SHALL NOT DIE. NONE OF HIS SINS THAT HE HATH COMMITTED SHALL BE MENTIONED UNTO HIM: HE HATH DONE THAT WHICH IS LAWFUL AND RIGHT; HE SHALL SURELY LIVE. YET THE CHILDREN OF THY PEOPLE SAY, THE WAY OF THE LORD IS NOT EQUAL: BUT AS FOR THEM, THEIR WAY IS NOT EQUAL. WHEN THE RIGHTEOUS TURNETH FROM HIS RIGHTEOUSNESS, AND COMMITTETH INIQUITY, HE SHALL DIE THEREBY. BUT IF THE WICKED TURN FROM HIS WICKEDNESS, AND DO THAT WHICH IS LAWFUL AND RIGHT, HE SHALL LIVE THEREBY. YET YE SAY, THE WAY OF THE LORD IS NOT EQUAL. O YE HOUSE OF ISRAEL, I WILL JUDGE YOU EVERY ONE AFTER HIS WAYS...Ezekiel 33:11-20 KJV.*

*Commentary~ Here the Lord explains that he will forgive a wicked man who repents of his evil and starts doing good. All his past sins will be forgotten. However, the rest of this scripture is even more interesting. God also teaches us that *if a righteous man does evil, all his righteousness will not be remembered.* All the past good things he did will not count once he starts doing evil, and he will die for his sin.

*DRAW NIGH TO GOD, AND HE WILL DRAW NIGH TO YOU. CLEANSE YOUR HANDS, YE SINNERS; AND PURIFY YOUR HEARTS, YE DOUBLE MINDED. BE AFFLICTED, AND MOURN, AND WEEP: LET YOUR LAUGHTER BE TURNED TO MOURNING, AND YOUR JOY TO HEAVINESS. **HUMBLE YOURSELVES IN THE SIGHT OF THE LORD**, AND HE SHALL LIFT YOUR UP....James 4:8-10 KJV.*

*SEEK YE THE LORD WHILE HE MAY BE FOUND, CALL YE UPON HIM WHILE HE IS NEAR: **LET THE WICKED FORSAKE HIS WAY**, AND THE UNRIGHTEOUS MAN HIS THOUGHTS: AND LET HIM RETURN UNTO THE LORD, AND HE WILL HAVE MERCY UPON HIM; AND TO OUR GOD, FOR HE WILL ABUNDANTLY PARDON...Isaiah 55:6-7 KJV.*

*IF THAT NATION, AGAINST WHOM I HAVE PRONOUNCED, **TURN FROM THEIR EVIL**, I WILL REPENT OF THE EVIL THAT I THOUGHT TO DO UNTO THEM. AND AT WHAT INSTANT I SHALL SPEAK CONCERNING A NATION, AND CONCERNING A KINGDOM, TO BUILD AND TO PLANT IT: IF IT DO EVIL IN MY SIGHT, THAT IT OBEY NOT MY VOICE,*

THEN I WILL REPENT OF THE GOOD, WHEREWITH I SAID I WOULD BENEFIT THEM. NOW THEREFORE GO TO, SPEAK TO THE MEN OF JUDAH, AND TO THE INHABITANTS OF JERUSALEM, SAYING, THUS SAITH THE LORD: BEHOLD, I FRAME EVIL AGAINST YOU, AND DEVISE A DEVICE AGAINST YOU: **RETURN YE NOW EVERY ONE FROM HIS EVIL WAY, AND MAKE YOUR WAYS AND YOUR DOINGS GOOD**...*Jeremiah 18:8-11 KJV.*

THUS SAITH THE LORD; STAND IN THE COURT OF THE LORD'S HOUSE, AND SPEAK UNTO ALL THE CITIES OF JUDAH, WHICH COME TO WORSHIP IN THE LORD'S HOUSE, ALL THE WORDS THAT I COMMAND THEE TO SPEAK UNTO THEM; DIMINISH NOT A WORD: IF SO BE THEY WILL HEARKEN, AND **TURN EVERY MAN FROM HIS EVIL WAY,** *THAT I MAY REPENT ME OF THE EVIL, WHICH I PURPOSE TO DO UNTO THEM BECAUSE OF THE EVIL OF THEIR DOINGS. AND THOU SHALT SAY UNTO THEM, THUS SAITH THE LORD; IF YE WILL NOT HEARKEN TO ME, TO WALK IN MY LAW, WHICH I HAVE SET BEFORE YOU, TO HEARKEN TO THE WORDS OF MY SERVANTS THE PROPHETS, WHOM I SENT UNTO YOU, BOTH RISING UP EARLY, AND SENDING THEM, BUT YE HAVE NOT HEARKENED; THEN WILL I MAKE THIS HOUSE LIKE SHILOH, AND WILL MAKE THIS CITY A CURSE TO ALL THE NATIONS OF THE EARTH...Jeremiah 26:2-6 KJV.*

REPENT YE THEREFORE, *AND BE CONVERTED, THAT YOUR SINS MAY BE BLOTTED OUT, WHEN THE TIMES*

OF REFRESHING SHALL COME FROM THE PRESENCE OF THE LORD…Acts 3:19 KJV.

IF WE SAY THAT WE HAVE NO SIN, WE DECEIVE OURSELVES, AND THE TRUTH IS NOT IN US. **IF WE CONFESS OUR SINS**, HE IS FAITHFUL AND JUST TO FORGIVE US OUR SINS, AND TO CLEANSE US FROM ALL UNRIGHTEOUSNESS…1John 1:8-9 KJV.

I ACKNOWLEDGED MY SIN UNTO THEE, AND MINE INIQUITY HAVE I NOT HID. I SAID, I WILL CONFESS MY TRANSGRESSIONS UNTO THE LORD; AND THOU FORGAVEST THE INIQUITY OF MY SIN. SELAH…Psalm 32:5 KJV.

HE THAT COVERETH HIS SINS SHALL NOT PROSPER: BUT WHOSO **CONFESSETH AND FORSAKETH** THEM SHALL HAVE MERCY…Proverbs 28:13 KJV.

IF THEY SIN AGAINST THEE, (FOR THERE IS NO MAN THAT SINNETH NOT,) AND THOU BE ANGRY WITH THEM, AND DELIVER THEM TO THE ENEMY, SO THAT THEY CARRY THEM AWAY CAPTIVES UNTO THE LAND OF THE ENEMY, FAR OR NEAR: YET IF THEY SHALL BETHINK THEMSELVES IN THE LAND WHITHER THEY WERE CARRIED CAPTIVES, AND **REPENT, AND MAKE SUPPLICATION UNTO THEE**

IN THE LAND OF THEM THAT CARRIED THEM CAPTIVES, SAYING, WE HAVE SINNED, AND HAVE DONE PERVERSELY, WE HAVE COMMITTED WICKEDNESS: AND SO RETURN UNTO THEE WITH ALL THEIR HEART, AND WITH ALL THEIR SOUL, *IN THE LAND OF THEIR ENEMIES, WHICH LED THEM AWAY CAPTIVE, AND PRAY UNTO THEE TOWARD THEIR LAND, WHICH THOU GAVEST UNTO THEIR FATHERS, THE CITY WHICH THOU HAST CHOSEN, AND THE HOUSE WHICH I HAVE BUILT FOR THY NAME: THEN HEAR THOU THEIR PRAYER AND THEIR SUPPLICATION IN HEAVEN THY DWELLING PLACE, AND MAINTAIN THEIR CAUSE, AND FORGIVE THY PEOPLE THAT HAVE SINNED AGAINST THEE, AND ALL THEIR TRANSGRESSIONS WHEREIN THEY HAVE TRANSGRESSED AGAINST THEE, AND GIVE THEM COMPASSION BEFORE THEM WHO CARRIED THEM CAPTIVE, THAT THEY MAY HAVE COMPASSION ON THEM…1Kings 8:46-50 KJV.*

IF MY PEOPLE, WHICH ARE CALLED BY MY NAME, SHALL HUMBLE THEMSELVES, AND PRAY, AND SEEK MY FACE, AND **TURN FROM THEIR WICKED WAYS**; *THEN I WILL HEAR FROM HEAVEN, AND WILL FORGIVE THEIR SIN, AND WILL HEAL THEIR LAND…2Chronicles 7:14 KJV.*

AND THE TIMES OF THIS IGNORANCE GOD WINKED AT; BUT NOW **COMMANDETH ALL MEN EVERY WHERE TO REPENT***…Acts 17:30 KJV.*

Context~ AND THE TIMES OF THIS IGNORANCE GOD WINKED AT: BUT NOW COMMANDETH ALL

MEN EVERYWHERE TO REPENT. BECAUSE HE HATH APPOINTED A DAY, IN WHICH HE WILL JUDGE THE WORLD IN RIGHTEOUSNESS BY THAT MAN WHOM HE HATH ORDAINED; WHEREOF HE HATH GIVEN ASSURANCE UNTO ALL MEN, IN THAT HE HATH RAISED HIM FROM THE DEAD. AND WHEN THEY HEARD OF THE RESURRECTION OF THE DEAD, SOME MOCKED: AND OTHERS SAID, WE WILL HEAR THEE AGAIN OF THIS MATTER. **SO PAUL DEPARTED FROM AMONG THEM**...*Acts 17:30-33 KJV.*

*Commentary~ Now that God has sent his Son to die for our sins, man's ignorance is no longer an excuse. All are commanded to repent. When people did not listen to Paul about repentance, he gave up and left them. He did not continue trying to speak to fools.

I TELL YOU, NAY: BUT, **EXCEPT YE REPENT**, *YE SHALL ALL LIKEWISE PERISH*...*Luke 13:3 and Luke 13:5 KJV.*

BUT WHEN HE SAW MANY OF THE PHARISEES AND SADDUCEES COME TO HIS BAPTISM, HE SAID UNTO THEM, O GENERATION OF VIPERS, WHO HATH WARNED YOU TO FLEE FROM THE WRATH TO COME? **BRING FORTH THEREFORE FRUITS MEET FOR REPENTANCE...**Matthew 3:7-8 KJV.*

REMEMBER THEREFORE HOW THOU HAST RECEIVED AND HEARD, AND HOLD FAST, **AND REPENT**. *IF*

THEREFORE THOU SHALT NOT WATCH, I WILL COME ON THEE AS A THIEF, AND THOU SHALT NOT KNOW WHAT HOUR I WILL COME UPON THEE. THOU HAST A FEW NAMES EVEN IN SARDIS WHICH HAVE NOT DEFILED THEIR GARMENTS; AND THEY SHALL WALK WITH ME IN WHITE: FOR THEY ARE WORTHY. HE THAT OVERCOMETH, THE SAME SHALL BE CLOTHED IN WHITE RAIMENT; AND I WILL NOT BLOT OUT HIS NAME OUT OF THE BOOK OF LIFE, BUT I WILL CONFESS HIS NAME BEFORE MY FATHER, AND BEFORE HIS ANGELS… Revelation 3:3-5 KJV.

*NOW AFTER THAT JOHN WAS PUT IN PRISON, JESUS CAME INTO GALILEE, PREACHING THE GOSPEL OF THE KINGDOM OF GOD, AND SAYING, THE TIME IS FULFILLED, AND THE KINGDOM OF GOD IS AT HAND: **REPENT YE**, AND BELIEVE THE GOSPEL…Mark 1:14-15 KJV.*

*AS MANY AS I LOVE, I REBUKE AND CHASTEN: BE ZEALOUS THEREFORE, AND **REPENT**…Revelation 3:19 KJV.*

*DELIVERING THEE FROM THE PEOPLE, AND FROM THE GENTILES, UNTO WHOM I NOW SEND THEE, **TO OPEN THEIR EYES, AND TO TURN THEM FROM DARKNESS TO LIGHT, AND FROM THE POWER OF SATAN UNTO GOD, THAT THEY MAY RECEIVE FORGIVENESS OF***

SINS, AND INHERITANCE AMONG THEM WHICH ARE SANCTIFIED BY FAITH THAT IS IN ME. WHEREUPON, O KING AGRIPPA, I WAS NOT DISOBEDIENT UNTO THE HEAVENLY VISION: BUT SHEWED FIRST UNTO THEM OF DAMASCUS, AND AT JERUSALEM, AND THROUGHOUT ALL THE COASTS OF JUDAEA, AND THEN TO THE GENTILES, THAT THEY SHOULD REPENT AND TURN TO GOD, AND DO WORKS MEET FOR REPENTANCE...Acts 26:17-20 KJV.

*I CAME NOT TO CALL THE RIGHTEOUS, **BUT SINNERS TO REPENTANCE**...Luke 5:32 KJV.*

***AND THAT REPENTANCE AND REMISSION OF SINS** SHOULD BE PREACHED IN HIS NAME AMONG ALL NATIONS, BEGINNING AT JERUSALEM...Luke 24:47 KJV.*

***REPENT** THEREFORE OF THIS THY WICKEDNESS, AND PRAY GOD, IF PERHAPS THE THOUGHT OF THINE HEART MAY BE FORGIVEN THEE...Acts 8:22 KJV.*

FOR REBELLION IS AS THE SIN OF WITCHCRAFT, AND STUBBORNNESS IS AS INIQUITY AND IDOLATRY. BECAUSE THOU HAST REJECTED THE WORD OF THE LORD, HE HATH ALSO REJECTED THEE FROM BEING KING. AND SAUL SAID UNTO SAMUEL, I HAVE SINNED:

*FOR I HAVE TRANSGRESSED THE COMMANDMENT OF THE LORD, AND THY WORDS: BECAUSE I FEARED THE PEOPLE, AND OBEYED THEIR VOICE. NOW THEREFORE, I PRAY THEE, PARDON MY SIN, AND TURN AGAIN WITH ME, THAT I MAY WORSHIP THE LORD. AND SAMUEL SAID UNTO SAUL, **I WILL NOT RETURN WITH THEE: FOR THOU HAST REJECTED THE WORD OF THE LORD, AND THE LORD HATH REJECTED THEE** FROM BEING KING OVER ISRAEL...1Samuel 15:23-26 KJV.*

*Commentary~ Saul was not genuinely remorseful for his sin. He was only "repenting" because the Lord was not allowing him to be king. He was also blaming "the people" for his sin instead of taking responsibility for it. Because his repentance was not godly, but selfish and self-serving, it was not accepted by either Samuel or God. This verse again teaches us that *phony, insincere repentance, given lip service only to benefit the offender, is not acceptable or deserving of forgiveness.*

Chapter 3

Things the Bible Says Specifically About Forgiving Another Believer

As you read on, notice that there are far fewer verses telling us to forgive than there were telling us to repent. It is interesting that the children of Satan manage to skip over all the verses on repentance (see previous chapter) whenever they decide to lecture us on forgiveness.

We have already established that the biblical formula for forgiveness which the Lord models for us and which Jesus teaches is repentance first, and then forgiveness. The following verses talk about forgiving; however, note *they do not eliminate the prerequisite of repentance*. There is no need to repeat it in these verses because it has already been established.

Almost every scripture about man's forgiveness is specifically referring to forgiving another believer. These were taught to avoid divisions in the young church and allow it to grow. *Remember that any time a scripture mentions your "brother," it is talking about a fellow member of the body of Christ.* It is not referring to unbelievers, and certainly not to the wicked or the wolves in sheep's clothing who claim to be Christian, but whose fruit gives them away. Remember that *people who abuse or betray other people are not true believers and are wicked; therefore, these verses do not pertain to them:*

*TAKE HEED TO YOURSELVES: IF **THY BROTHER** TRESPASS AGAINST THEE, REBUKE HIM; AND **IF HE REPENT**, FORGIVE HIM...Luke 17:3 KJV.*

*LET ALL BITTERNESS, AND WRATH, AND ANGER, AND CLAMOUR, AND EVIL SPEAKING, BE PUT AWAY FROM YOU, WITH ALL MALICE. AND BE YE KIND ONE TO ANOTHER, TENDERHEARTED, FORGIVING **ONE ANOTHER**, EVEN AS GOD FOR CHRIST'S SAKE HATH FORGIVEN YOU....Ephesians 4:31-32 KJV.*

Context~ I THEREFORE, THE PRISONER OF THE LORD, BESEECH YOU THAT YE WALK WORTHY OF THE VOCATION WHEREWITH YE ARE CALLED, WITH ALL LOWLINESS AND MEEKNESS, WITH LONGSUFFERING, FORBEARING **ONE ANOTHER IN LOVE; ENDEAVOURING TO **KEEP THE UNITY** OF THE SPIRIT IN THE BOND OF PEACE. THERE IS ONE BODY, AND ONE SPIRIT, EVEN AS YE ARE CALLED IN ONE HOPE OF YOUR CALLING; ONE LORD, ONE FAITH, ONE BAPTISM, ONE GOD AND FATHER OF ALL, WHO IS ABOVE ALL, AND THROUGH ALL, AND IN YOU ALL...Ephesians 4:1-6 KJV.*

*Commentary~ Note at the beginning of Ephesians and in the context above who Paul is talking to. He is addressing the saints of God in the church in Ephesus (Ephesians 1:1) and exhorting them to stay united as one body and one Spirit, and avoid divisions within the young church so that it can grow. *This scripture is*

not a teaching on being tenderhearted and forgiving toward the wicked, only to brothers and sisters in Christ.

FORBEARING ONE ANOTHER, AND FORGIVING ONE ANOTHER, IF ANY MAN HAVE A QUARREL AGAINST ANY: EVEN AS CHRIST FORGAVE YOU, SO ALSO DO YE...*Colossians 3:13 KJV.*

*Context~ PUT ON THEREFORE, AS THE ELECT OF GOD, HOLY AND BELOVED, BOWELS OF MERCIES, KINDNESS, HUMBLENESS OF MIND, MEEKNESS, LONGSUFFERING; FORBEARING **ONE ANOTHER**, AND FORGIVING **ONE ANOTHER**, IF ANY MAN HAVE A QUARREL AGAINST ANY: EVEN AS CHRIST FORGAVE YOU, SO ALSO DO YE. AND ABOVE ALL THESE THINGS PUT ON CHARITY, WHICH IS THE BOND OF PERFECTNESS. AND LET THE PEACE OF GOD RULE IN YOUR HEARTS, TO THE WHICH ALSO **YE ARE CALLED IN ONE BODY**; AND BE YE THANKFUL. LET THE WORD OF CHRIST DWELL IN YOU RICHLY IN ALL WISDOM; TEACHING AND **ADMONISHING ONE ANOTHER** IN PSALMS AND HYMNS AND SPIRITUAL SONGS, SINGING WITH GRACE IN YOUR HEARTS TO THE LORD...Colossians 3:12-16 KJV.*

*Commentary~ Here Paul is addressing the saints and fellow believers in Christ at Colosse (Colossians 1:1-2), referring to settling differences between fellow believers, to foster unity in the body of Christ. Notice the instruction to admonish one another, not to keep silent.

*Additional Commentary~ Note also that Paul's instruction to be "longsuffering," which is frequently used against us by abuse-enablers, is not pertaining to forgiving the wicked, only to forgiving the children of God. It simply means to be patient with our sisters and brothers in Christ. I find it interesting that although abusers and their Flying Monkeys tell us the Bible says to be "longsuffering," they never tell us that it also says not to associate with the wicked. Why obey one and ignore the other? If we shun the children of Satan, as we are instructed to do, this will eliminate most of the "longsuffering" in our lives, ungodly suffering we were never meant to bear. The Bible is not telling us that it is virtuous to suffer for decades at the hands of the evil. We were supposed to have already eliminated them from our lives. Whatever "patience" we will need to get along with genuine Christians will not try us half as much as what we would need to get along with demonic people. God never meant for us to need that much patience.

*BUT IF ANYONE HAS CAUSED GRIEF, HE HAS NOT GRIEVED ME, BUT ALL OF YOU TO SOME EXTENT- NOT TO BE TOO SEVERE. THIS PUNISHMENT WHICH WAS INFLICTED BY THE MAJORITY IS SUFFICIENT FOR SUCH A MAN, SO THAT, ON THE CONTRARY, YOU OUGHT RATHER TO **FORGIVE AND COMFORT HIM, LEST PERHAPS SUCH A ONE BE SWALLOWED UP WITH TOO MUCH SORROW.** THEREFORE I URGE YOU TO REAFFIRM YOUR LOVE TO HIM. FOR TO THIS END I ALSO WROTE, THAT I MIGHT PUT YOU TO THE TEST, WHETHER YOU ARE OBEDIENT IN ALL THINGS. NOW WHOM YOU FORGIVE ANYTHING, I ALSO FORGIVE. FOR IF INDEED I HAVE FORGIVEN ANYTHING, I HAVE FORGIVEN THAT ONE FOR YOUR SAKES IN THE PRESENCE OF CHRIST, LEST SATAN SHOULD TAKE ADVANTAGE OF US; FOR WE ARE NOT IGNORANT OF HIS DEVICES....2Corinthians 2:5-8 NKJV.*

*Commentary~ Here Paul is addressing the church in Corinth about church discipline. He is not talking about forgiving out-siders or the evil. Paul is not saying that causing grief to others should have no consequences; he says that the majority in the church should decide on an appropriate punishment. He is also saying to offer forgiveness and love to a fellow believer who is so remorseful and repentant about what he did that he is in dan-ger of being overcome by his sorrow. He is not saying to forgive someone who is unrepentant.

Chapter 4

Things the Bible Says About Forgiveness That Do Not Specify the Forgiveness of a Fellow Believer

There are only two verses that talk about forgiveness without being specific about it being toward another believer. *Note these verses do not eliminate the already established protocol of repentance first.* Yes, we are required to forgive men their trespasses when they have repented, just like our Father forgives us when we have repented.

> AND WHEN YE STAND PRAYING, FORGIVE, IF YE HAVE OUGHT AGAINST ANY: THAT YOUR FATHER ALSO WHICH IS IN HEAVEN MAY FORGIVE YOU YOUR TRESPASSES. BUT IF YE DO NOT FORGIVE, NEITHER WILL YOUR FATHER WHICH IS IN HEAVEN FORGIVE YOUR TRESPASSES...Mark 11:24-25 KJV.

*Commentary~ No verse eliminates the requirement for repentance, even if it is not specifically mentioned. Even if you do forgive another person, your Father would still not forgive you if you did not repent of your own sins and if you fully intended to keep on sinning. That is just common sense, and it is also taught repeatedly in the Bible. So when we stand praying, if we still have anything against anyone *who has repented* of what they did to us, we must forgive them or our Father will withhold his forgiveness from us. We are still not, however, under any obligation to forgive someone who has not repented.

AND FORGIVE US OUR DEBTS, AS WE FORGIVE OUR DEBTORS...Matthew 6:12 KJV.

*Context~ AND FORGIVE US OUR DEBTS, AS WE FORGIVE OUR DEBTORS. AND LEAD US NOT INTO TEMPTATION, BUT DELIVER US FROM EVIL: FOR THINE IS THE KINGDOM, AND THE POWER, AND THE GLORY, FOR EVER. AMEN. FOR IF YE FORGIVE MEN THEIR TRESPASSES, YOUR HEAVENLY FATHER WILL ALSO FORGIVE YOU: BUT IF YE FORGIVE NOT MEN THEIR TRESPASSES, NEITHER WILL YOUR FATHER FORGIVE YOUR TRESPASSES....Matthew 6:12-15 KJV.

*Commentary~ Again, even if we do forgive, we still would not be forgiven unless we also repent. Our forgiveness of others does not eliminate the requirement for us to repent of our own sins. When we repent, God forgives us, and he does not expect more of us than he himself is willing to do. To think otherwise is to believe that we are supposed to be "holier" than God. See the next chapter for a more in-depth study of Matthew.

Chapter 5

Matthew's Gospel: The Chapter Most Often Used by the Wicked to Pressure Victims to Forgive

Matthew's gospel is frequently used by abusers and their enablers against those who try to confront their wickedness. They cherry-pick verses they remember and then, as usual, only read half the verse or conveniently skip over the context. In this chapter, we will take a closer look at several of these passages.

It is again important to note that almost all of these verses specifically refer to settling disagreements with a "brother," in order to allow the young church to thrive and grow without divisions. *That does not mean that Jesus wants us to have fewer (or no) requirements for forgiving a child of Satan than he wants us to have for forgiving a fellow Christian.* That would be insane. It means that *Jesus is not interested in us reconciling with the evil,* and does not feel the need to preach about it.

The scripture that is probably used most often by Holier-Than-Thous who are trying to shame us for not being their idea of "good Christians" by not forgiving on demand is Matthew 7:1-5 (This verse is repeated almost word for word in Luke 6:37-42):

*JUDGE NOT, THAT YE BE NOT JUDGED. FOR WITH WHAT JUDGMENT YE JUDGE, YE SHALL BE JUDGED: AND WITH WHAT MEASURE YE METE, IT SHALL BE MEASURED TO YOU AGAIN. AND WHY BEHOLDEST THOU THE MOTE THAT IS IN **THY BROTHER'S** EYE, BUT CONSIDEREST NOT THE BEAM THAT IS IN THINE OWN EYE? OR HOW WILT THOU SAY TO THY BROTHER, LET ME PULL OUT THE MOTE OUT OF THINE EYE; AND BEHOLD, A BEAM IS IN THINE OWN EYE? **THOU HYPOCRITE, FIRST** CAST OUT THE BEAM OUT OF THINE OWN EYE; AND **THEN** SHALT THOU SEE CLEARLY TO CAST OUT THE MOTE OUT OF THY BROTHER'S EYE....Matthew 7:1-5 KJV.*

*Commentary~ Note this passage clearly tells us to *first* cast the beam out of our own eye, and *then* we can see clearly to cast the mote out of our brother's eye. It does not tell us *not to* cast the mote out of our brother's eye. It tells us to *examine ourselves first and not be hypocrites*, living wickedly while pompously judging *our fellow believers in Christ* (like those phony Holier-Than-Thous who judge *us*). It does not mean not to judge the world or the wicked, because the Bible clearly tells us that the saints of God are to judge those. It is also not telling us to *never* rebuke a fellow believer; it is simply telling us to make sure *we* are righteous first, so that we can see clearly and judge justly. Take a look at the following verse:

*I SAY UNTO YOU, THAT LIKEWISE JOY SHALL BE IN HEAVEN OVER ONE SINNER THAT REPENTETH, MORE THAN OVER NINETY AND NINE **JUST PERSONS, WHICH NEED NO REPENTANCE**...Luke 15:7 KJV.*

*Commentary~ This is a very interesting answer to those who use Matthew 7:1-5 (and Luke 6:41-42) against us when we confront their evil. Note that the righteous do not have "beams in their eyes." They need no repentance, because they have already repented. *Matthew 7:1-5 and Luke 6:41-42 were not addressed to the righteous. They were addressed to hypocrites.*

BUT I SAY UNTO YOU, THAT YE RESIST NOT EVIL: BUT WHOSOEVER SHALL SMITE THEE ON THY RIGHT CHEEK, TURN TO HIM THE OTHER ALSO...Matthew 5:39 KJV.

*Context ~ YE HAVE HEARD THAT IT HATH BEEN SAID, AN EYE FOR AN EYE, AND A TOOTH FOR A TOOTH: BUT I SAY UNTO YOU, THAT YE RESIST NOT EVIL: BUT WHOSOEVER SHALL SMITE THEE ON THY RIGHT CHEEK, TURN TO HIM THE OTHER ALSO....Matthew 5:38-39 KJV.

*Commentary~ Jesus is telling us not to take revenge, not to take the eye for an eye or the tooth for a tooth specified in the Old Testament. He is not telling us not to defend ourselves or our loved ones. He is simply telling us not to retaliate, because vengeance is the Lord's (Deuteronomy 32:35; Romans 12:19). Note that merely staying away from someone (called shunning and taught in the New Testament as well as the Old Testament) is *not* "taking revenge." There is more to this scripture in the cultural context of the times. Do an internet search for "turn the other cheek" and you will find explanations of what it really meant to "turn the other cheek" in Jesus' time.

*THEREFORE IF THOU BRING THY GIFT TO THE ALTAR, AND THERE REMEMBEREST **THAT THY BROTHER HATH OUGHT AGAINST THEE**; LEAVE THERE THY GIFT BEFORE THE ALTAR, AND GO THY WAY; FIRST*

BE RECONCILED TO THY BROTHER, AND THEN COME AND OFFER THY GIFT...Matthew 5:23-24 KJV.

*Commentary~ This verse does not say "if *you* have something against your brother" go and forgive him, although abuse-defenders like to read it that way. It says "if your brother has something against *you*." That means *if you are the one who has wronged your brother* (causing him to have something against you), go and make amends with him before coming to God with your offerings. If someone has done evil to us, it is up to them to come to us and repent. It is not up to us to go to them and insist on reconciliation regardless of whether they are repentant or not. This is also another verse that is referring to a brother in the faith, not the wicked.

*BUT I SAY UNTO YOU, THAT WHOSOEVER IS ANGRY WITH HIS BROTHER **WITHOUT A CAUSE** SHALL BE IN DANGER OF THE JUDGMENT: AND WHOSOEVER SHALL SAY TO HIS BROTHER, RACA, SHALL BE IN DANGER OF THE COUNCIL: BUT WHOSOEVER SHALL SAY, THOU FOOL, SHALL BE IN DANGER OF HELL FIRE...Matthew 5:22 KJV.*

*Commentary~ This passage acknowledges that there is such a thing as righteous anger, and we will not be judged for that. It specifically says that anger *without a cause* is subject to judgment. Both Father God and Jesus showed righteous anger when it was appropriate. Again, it is referring to a genuine brother in Christ.

Here is another verse often used by abuse-enablers to pressure victims to forgive the same abuses over and over again:

*THEN CAME PETER TO HIM, AND SAID, LORD, HOW OFT SHALL **MY BROTHER** SIN AGAINST ME, AND I FORGIVE HIM? TILL SEVEN TIMES? JESUS SAITH UNTO HIM, I SAY NOT UNTO THEE, UNTIL SEVEN TIMES: BUT, UNTIL SEVENTY TIMES SEVEN...Matthew 18:21-22 KJV.*

*Context~ TAKE HEED THAT YE DESPISE NOT ONE OF THESE LITTLE ONES: FOR I SAY UNTO YOU, THAT IN HEAVEN THEIR ANGELS DO ALWAYS BEHOLD THE FACE OF MY FATHER WHICH IS IN HEAVEN. FOR THE SON OF MAN IS COME TO SAVE THAT WHICH WAS LOST. HOW THINK YE? IF A MAN HAVE AN HUNDRED SHEEP, AND ONE OF THEM BE GONE ASTRAY, DOTH HE NOT LEAVE THE NINETY AND NINE, AND GOETH INTO THE MOUNTAINS, AND SEEKETH THAT WHICH IS GONE ASTRAY? AND IF SO BE THAT HE FIND IT, VERILY I SAY UNTO YOU, HE REJOICETH MORE OF THAT SHEEP, THAN OF THE NINETY AND NINE WHICH WENT NOT ASTRAY. EVEN SO IT IS NOT THE WILL OF YOUR FATHER WHICH IS IN HEAVEN, THAT ONE OF THESE LITTLE ONES SHOULD PERISH...Matthew 18: 10-14 KJV.

*Commentary~ God does not want anyone to die in their sin. This is what the requirement of repentance is meant to accomplish. By not holding the wicked accountable and requiring that they turn from their wicked ways before we forgive them, we are cheapening forgiveness and also taking away an incentive for them to stop doing evil and turn to God. In Matthew 18:21-22, Jesus is giving Peter an instruction for forgiving new, "baby (milk-fed)" believers when they repent, lest they become discouraged and leave the church. It is not God's will that one of these "little ones," who can be brought back by a spirit of repentance, should perish.

> *Additional Context~ MOREOVER IF **THY BROTHER** SHALL TRESPASS AGAINST THEE, GO AND TELL HIM HIS FAULT BETWEEN THEE AND HIM ALONE: IF HE SHALL HEAR THEE, THOU HAST GAINED THY BROTHER. BUT IF HE WILL NOT HEAR THEE, THEN TAKE WITH THEE ONE OR TWO MORE, THAT IN THE MOUTH OF TWO OR THREE WITNESSES EVERY WORD MAY BE ESTABLISHED. AND IF HE SHALL NEGLECT TO HEAR THEM, TELL IT UNTO THE CHURCH: BUT IF HE NEGLECT TO HEAR THE CHURCH, **LET HIM BE UNTO THEE AS AN HEATHEN MAN AND A PUBLICAN. VERILY I SAY UNTO YOU, WHATSOEVER YE SHALL BIND ON EARTH SHALL BE BOUND IN HEAVEN: AND WHATSOEVER YE SHALL LOOSE ON EARTH SHALL BE LOOSED IN HEAVEN.** AGAIN, I SAY UNTO YOU, THAT IF TWO OF YOU SHALL AGREE ON EARTH AS TOUCHING ANY THING THAT THEY SHALL ASK, IT SHALL BE DONE FOR THEM OF MY FATHER WHICH IS IN HEAVEN. FOR WHERE TWO OR THREE ARE GATHERED TOGETHER IN MY NAME, THERE AM I IN THE MIDST OF THEM. THEN CAME PETER TO HIM, AND SAID, LORD, HOW OFT SHALL MY BROTHER SIN AGAINST ME, AND I FORGIVE HIM? TILL SEVEN TIMES? JESUS SAITH UNTO HIM, I SAY NOT UNTO THEE, UNTIL SEVEN TIMES: BUT UNTIL SEVENTY TIMES SEVEN…Matthew 18:15-22.

*Commentary~ Again, this scripture refers to a *brother*~ a fellow believer. It is another instruction to settle disputes *within the church*, not with the evil. Obviously we cannot bring a dispute with a wicked person to the church because church elders or members and their opinions do not matter to him. Note we are told to treat an unrepentant brother as a heathen and a publican (shun him). If Jesus gives us these instructions for a fellow believer, how much more (not less) would they apply to a child of the devil? Most of us have never seen an abuser truly repent even one time, much less seventy times seven, so this scripture will pretty much never apply to our situations with narcissists, psychopaths and other abusive people.

*Additional Commentary~ It is very interesting that Jesus tells us that whatever we bind on earth will be bound in heaven and what we loose on earth will be loosed in heaven. This is said in the context of forgiveness. If we are left with no choice but to treat the one who has trespassed against us as a heathen or a publican (not forgive him, but shun him), because of his own refusal to hear our complaint and repent of what he has done to us, *then God in heaven comes into agreement with us* and does not forgive him either. This is an amazing, validating, rarely known part of Matthew 18, and usually conveniently overlooked by abusers and abuse-defenders.

Matthew 18 continues with a parable~

*THEREFORE IS THE KINGDOM OF HEAVEN LIKENED UNTO A CERTAIN KING, WHICH WOULD TAKE ACCOUNT OF HIS SERVANTS, AND WHEN HE HAD BEGUN TO RECKON, ONE WAS BROUGHT UNTO HIM, WHICH OWED HIM TEN THOUSAND TALENTS. BUT FORASMUCH AS HE HAD NOT TO PAY, HIS LORD COMMANDED HIM TO BE SOLD, AND HIS WIFE, AND CHILDREN, AND ALL THAT HE HAD, AND PAYMENT TO BE MADE. **THE SERVANT THEREFORE FELL DOWN AND WORSHIPPED HIM, SAYING, LORD, HAVE***

PATIENCE WITH ME, AND I WILL PAY THEE ALL.
THEN THE LORD OF THAT SERVANT WAS MOVED WITH
COMPASSION, AND LOOSED HIM, AND FORGAVE HIM
THE DEBT. BUT THE SAME SERVANT WENT OUT, AND
FOUND ONE OF HIS FELLOWSERVANTS, WHICH OWED
HIM AN HUNDRED PENCE: AND HE LAID HANDS ON
HIM, AND TOOK HIM BY THE THROAT, SAYING, PAY ME
THAT THOU OWEST. AND HIS FELLOWSERVANT FELL
DOWN AT HIS FEET, AND BESOUGHT HIM, SAYING,
HAVE PATIENCE WITH ME, AND I WILL PAY THEE ALL.
AND HE WOULD NOT: BUT WENT AND CAST HIM INTO
PRISON, TILL HE SHOULD PAY THE DEBT. SO WHEN HIS
FELLOWSERVANTS SAW WHAT WAS DONE, THEY WERE
VERY SORRY, AND CAME AND TOLD UNTO THEIR LORD
ALL THAT WAS DONE. THEN HIS LORD, AFTER THAT HE
HAD CALLED HIM, SAID UNTO HIM, O THOU WICKED
SERVANT, I FORGAVE THEE ALL THAT DEBT, BECAUSE
THOU DESIREDST ME: SHOULDEST NOT THOU ALSO
HAVE HAD COMPASSION ON THY FELLOWSERVANT,
EVEN AS I HAD PITY ON THEE? AND HIS LORD WAS
WROTH, AND DELIVERED HIM TO THE TORMENTORS,
TILL HE SHOULD PAY ALL THAT WAS DUE UNTO HIM.
SO LIKEWISE SHALL MY HEAVENLY FATHER DO ALSO
UNTO YOU, IF YE FROM YOUR HEARTS FORGIVE NOT
EVERY ONE ***HIS BROTHER*** *THEIR TRESPASSES....*
Matthew 18: 23-35 KJV.

*Commentary~ The servant fell down and begged for mercy. He did not deny his debt, lie about it, blame anyone else, etc. *He admitted it and promised to make it right.* His master forgave him, but when he found out his servant was not similarly merciful to the one who owed him, *he recanted his forgiveness and reinstated his punishment.* This parable does not say we must forgive those who do not repent; in fact, it says that it is just to withhold our mercy from those who withhold their mercy from others (abuse is one example of a lack of mercy). It explains that we are to forgive someone *when they repent of what they have done*, or our heavenly Father will not forgive us *when we repent*. But if they continue in their evil, we are justified in not forgiving them. It also explains that if, at some point after we have forgiven them, they revert to their old wicked selves and do evil again, we are justified in retracting our forgiveness.

Chapter 6

Things the Bible Never Says

These statements are often made by fake holier-than-thou "Christians" to pressure victims to forgive. Many times, they are spoken of as if they were in the Bible, as in, "God wants us to forgive and forget," or "the Bible says we have to let bygones be bygones." The Bible says nothing of the kind, and fake "Christians" do not speak for God. You will not find any of these platitudes and misconceptions in the Bible:

* Forgive and forget
* Be the bigger person
* Let bygones be bygones
* That's all in the past
* Everybody deserves another chance
* Forgiveness means you have to reconcile the relationship
* When you forgive someone you have to tell her you forgave her
* You have to let other people know whether or not you've forgiven someone
* You have to forgive right away
* You have to forgive as soon as it's asked for or demanded
* Christians are not supposed to get angry

* Christians are supposed to lie about or cover up evil
* Christians should not talk about what was done to them
* You have to forgive anyone who apologizes
* An apology means the person repented
* God forgives everyone

"Forgive and forget," along with most of the above statements, is used just as frequently, if not more so, by bystanders than offenders. "Forgiving and forgetting" will allow the group (family, social circle, church) where abuse has occurred to pretend nothing happened and continue with no disruption.

When someone uses any of the above clichés against a victim of abuse or treachery, what they are really saying is "I don't want you to rock the boat because then things will get complicated for me. As long as it's you being abused or stabbed in the back, and not me, I'm comfortable. Don't ask me to hold an abuser accountable, take sides, put myself in the line of fire to defend you, or go past my comfort zone." If you won't forget, you make the spineless abuse-enablers feel awkward. You will be perceived as the trouble-maker instead of the abuser, and will be shunned from the group.

Abuse-enablers also realize that if you stay away instead of "forgiving and forgetting" and getting back into line, they may become the abuser's next target because you are out of range. So although it may seem nervy and weird for some third party to butt into your dispute with another adult and tell you what you should do, consider if they actually have a stake in getting you to make up with the abuser. None of the above Nonsense Statements have anything to do with justice or with protecting the innocent. They are only about convenience, not rocking the boat, and keeping the status-quo. And God never said any of them.

Chapter 7

No Forgiveness for the Unrepentant

DO NOT I HATE THEM, O LORD, THAT HATE THEE? AND AM NOT I GRIEVED WITH THOSE THAT RISE UP AGAINST THEE? I HATE THEM WITH PERFECT HATRED: I COUNT THEM MINE ENEMIES. SEARCH ME, O GOD, AND KNOW MY HEART: TRY ME, AND KNOW MY THOUGHTS: AND SEE IF THERE BE ANY WICKED WAY IN ME, AND LEAD ME IN THE WAY EVERLASTING...Psalm 139:21-24 KJV.

Have you ever had it happen that when you rebuked an abuser, not only did she refuse to apologize, show the slightest bit of remorse, or change her hurtful behavior, but she then proceeded to smugly inform you that "God forgives her," because "God forgives everybody," and the Bible says that *you* have to forgive her, too? I have, more than once.

And all I can say to that is, "Nice try." Biblical forgiveness doesn't work that way. Not even close. As we learned in the scriptures we have already studied, God forgives those who *repent*, not people who don't repent and keep right on sinning. Repentance means turning from one's sinful ways and changing one's life. It does not mean continuing on as before, and it also does not mean stopping just one or two obnoxious behaviors while continuing all the rest, or even inventing some new ones. It might surprise such self-righteous offenders to learn that God does not forgive "everybody," and that he does not tell us to, either. In fact, *there is not one instance* in the Bible of the Lord forgiving anyone who remains "stiff-necked" (stubborn) and unrepentant and continues doing evil.

The idea that God "forgives everyone," whether they repent of their wickedness or not, is complete nonsense. If it were true, then there would be no need for hell. Everybody would be going to heaven. One doesn't even need to study the Bible to realize it says nothing of the kind. That's just common sense, and to believe such a thing is absurd.

Those who know the Lord and study his Word know that he has such a heart of love for the downtrodden and the broken-hearted, and that he desires us to be free of every kind of bondage. God's Word is infallible, and God does not play mean little tricks on abuse victims. He *never* says anything that would make it easier for a sinner to keep on sinning or an abuser to keep on abusing. To even suggest otherwise is to reveal a profound ignorance of God's divine nature.

Biblically speaking, *no one* gets forgiven without changing his ways and turning to God and godliness. The New Testament includes an additional requirement for meriting forgiveness- accepting Jesus as one's Lord and Savior. And the Bible teaches us that no one who has genuinely done that can continue abusing others (1 John 3:9-10). Abusers would just love an excuse to obligate us to forgive them without the slightest effort on their parts to make amends, commit to change, or have anything expected of them at all. It's an abuser's dream gig- to be able to commit one evil deed after another with impunity, and then pervert the Word of God by claiming that others have to repeatedly and unconditionally forgive her. This is utter nonsense:

BE NOT DECEIVED; GOD IS NOT MOCKED: FOR WHATSOEVER A MAN SOWETH, THAT SHALL HE ALSO REAP....Galatians 6:7 KJV.

The Bible is not an excuse for abusive people to have a field day without ever suffering any consequences. Distorting the Word of God to get away with evil is an indication of the demonic nature of such people, not of their innocence and good intentions. Ask any deliverance minister and you will learn that twisting God's Word to facilitate evil is one of the most common tactics used by demons.

Abusers, by definition, wouldn't have the slightest idea what the Bible *really* says about forgiveness, or anything else for that matter. It's not like they spend a lot of time studying the Word of God and applying it to their lives. They're just parroting something they heard somewhere along the line, and twisting it to suit their own purposes. Again, they can quote scripture, but have no understanding of the true spiritual meaning of what they reel off. They're using what they imagine the scriptures say to pressure us and guilt us into forgiving them, when they have done nothing whatsoever to deserve our forgiveness.

Some abusers like to call themselves "Christians" because it enables them to get away with abusive behavior more frequently without being challenged or confronted. These people might actually be familiar with the Bible, and then use it, twist it, and take it out of context to justify their behavior and attempt to deceive us into forgiving them when no forgiveness is warranted. But talk is cheap. We need to study God's Word concerning this, and pray for the discernment and wisdom to distinguish between *real* Christians and *pretend* Christians- those who are conveniently "Christian" only when it suits them. One big clue is that *real Christians **act like** real Christians*. This means they do not mistreat other people:

WHOSOEVER IS BORN OF GOD DOTH NOT COMMIT SIN; *FOR HIS SEED REMAINETH IN HIM: AND HE CANNOT SIN, BECAUSE HE IS BORN OF GOD.* **IN THIS THE CHILDREN OF GOD ARE MANIFEST, AND THE CHILDREN OF THE DEVIL: WHOSOEVER DOETH NOT RIGHTEOUSNESS IS NOT OF GOD,** *NEITHER HE THAT LOVETH NOT HIS BROTHER....1 John 3:9-10 KJV.*

The Bible does in fact tell us that we should forgive as the Lord forgave us (Colossians 3:13; Ephesians 4:32). But the Lord has requirements for forgiveness. If we read in more depth and in context about God forgiving us, including the hows, whys, and under what circumstances, we will see that he only forgives us when we come to him in the spirit of remorse, change our lives through his Son, ask for forgiveness, and repent (change). So if we are to forgive others as God forgives us, then we are to forgive them *after* they have shown genuine remorse by the grace of Jesus' cleansing blood, and *after* they have changed and stopped doing evil- *not before*. That is the formula for forgiveness which God models for us, and that is the formula which he instructs us to follow.

We are not supposed to render meaningless the blessing of forgiveness by giving it prematurely or undeservedly to those who demand it and act as if they are entitled to it, and yet have done nothing to merit it. As we have said, the Lord's higher purpose is to change men's hearts and make them turn from evil, give up their wicked ways, and choose to follow *him* instead of Satan. He does that by requiring repentance before forgiveness, not by giving evildoers a free ride.

In Luke 17:3, Jesus tells us very clearly that we are to forgive someone who sins against us *if* he repents. He does not tell us to forgive everyone, even those who have absolutely no remorse and fully intend to continue abusing others and behaving badly.

That would be preposterous and contradictory. God does not do nonsensical things that do not serve his ultimate purpose of bringing all men into his grace and his presence.

When an abuser refuses to change his ways, stop abusing, and start doing good, *then we are biblically unable to grant him forgiveness.* When we cannot forgive him because of his intention to continue repeating his evil, then God does not forgive him, either:

> *AGAIN JESUS SAID, "PEACE BE WITH YOU! AS THE FATHER HAS SENT ME, I AM SENDING YOU." AND WITH THAT HE BREATHED ON THEM AND SAID, "RECEIVE THE HOLY SPIRIT. **IF YOU FORGIVE ANYONE HIS SINS, THEY ARE FORGIVEN; IF YOU DO NOT FORGIVE THEM, THEY ARE NOT FORGIVEN**"....John 20:21-22 NIV.*

In this way, we, his saints, are acting as God's representatives. If we adhere to biblical principles when considering forgiveness, then we are restricted from forgiving our abusers as long as they continue their wicked, abusive (and therefore sinful) behavior. And if *we* cannot forgive them, then *God* does not forgive them either, despite what they might believe.

The Bible teaches us that all evil behavior has consequences. The only way to come into a state of grace is to give up sinfulness and walk in the ways of the Lord, in love for others. Abusers, by nature, could not care less about coming closer to God, and usually need some extra incentive to straighten up and fly right. That incentive is often some kind of social censure, which may, for a particular individual, include our refusal to forgive him until and if he has earned it.

There are times that God will use us in this way to bring a person into repentance and to him. By forgiving unremorseful evildoers, we are not helping them and we are not serving God's purposes. We are depriving them of the opportunity to repent and transform their lives, to truly accept Jesus as their Savior so their sins can be washed away, and to walk forever with our Father. By interfering with God's Law of Sowing and Reaping, we are preventing God's purpose from being fulfilled in that individual's life.

The Lord requires that we do our part in bringing others to repentance:

> SO THOU, O SON OF MAN, I HAVE SET THEE A WATCHMAN UNTO THE HOUSE OF ISRAEL; THEREFORE THOU SHALT HEAR THE WORD AT MY MOUTH, AND **WARN THEM FROM ME.** WHEN I SAY UNTO THE WICKED, O WICKED MAN, THOU SHALT SURELY DIE; IF THOU DOST NOT SPEAK TO WARN THE WICKED FROM HIS WAY, THAT WICKED MAN SHALL DIE IN HIS INIQUITY; BUT HIS BLOOD WILL I REQUIRE AT THINE HAND. NEVERTHELESS, IF THOU WARN THE WICKED OF HIS WAY TO TURN FROM IT; IF HE DO NOT TURN FROM HIS WAY, HE SHALL DIE IN HIS INIQUITY; BUT THOU HAST DELIVERED THY SOUL.....Ezekiel 33:7-9 KJV.

So despite attempts by ungodly people to mislead, deceive or pressure us, we need to stand firm in the knowledge that the Lord does *not* forgive those who are "stiff-necked," refuse to repent, and fully intend to continue in their sin- and he does not expect us to, either. There are *conditions* on receiving forgiveness, there is a *reason* for those conditions, and the conditions are repentance and turning from one's evil ways. Forgiveness is not to be given just because someone simply demands it or insists that he is entitled to it. It is only to be offered to those who are truly worthy of it.

Chapter 8

What About "Father, Forgive Them; For They Know Not What They Do?"

THEN SAID JESUS, FATHER, FORGIVE THEM; FOR THEY KNOW NOT WHAT THEY DO. AND THEY PARTED HIS RAIMENT AND CAST LOTS....LUKE 23:34 KJV.

Sometimes the basic teaching that there is no such thing as unconditional forgiveness in God's Word leads to disagreements with those who seem to feel that abusers should be able to continually cause pain for other people while smugly claiming that God forgives them and that their victims have to forgive them as well, even though they have done absolutely nothing to deserve forgiveness. And they are most fond of citing Jesus' words to our Father God, asking for the forgiveness of those who persecuted him even though they did not repent.

Many victims have experienced their abusers and enablers using this scripture to pressure them to forgive when no forgiveness is merited. The devil just loves to cause confusion. But whenever we are trying to understand an apparent contradiction in the Bible, the Holy Spirit will illuminate it for us and give us the insight we ask for. Thank you, Lord!

To begin with, it is interesting to note that the footnotes in the versions of the Bible which include footnotes (NIV, NLT, NASB, etc.) state that many ancient manuscripts do not contain this verse. This calls into question whether or not Jesus even said it, or if it was simply added later by men who translated and compiled the scriptures and decided it should be there.

Additionally, out of all four accounts of Jesus' death in the four gospels, only Luke makes mention of this remark of Jesus'. Most scholars believe that Luke was not present at the crucifixion and did not know Jesus personally but became an apostle after Jesus' death, because he traveled with Paul too many years later for his gospel to be a first-hand account of the crucifixion. If indeed The Lord actually said this sentence, it is interesting and perhaps relevant that none of the other apostles thought it was significant enough to mention in their otherwise meticulous recordings of Jesus' teachings. Luke might have included it simply to make sure his account of our Lord's crucifixion was as complete as he thought possible, or it may not have been accurately relayed to him.

At any rate, the apostles who were there and witnessed Jesus' death first hand were in a much better position to judge his intentions at the time than we are two thousand years later. They might not have all felt that this particular comment of our Lord's was something he meant for them to document and pass down to us as a teaching. Therefore, I believe we need to consider whether we might possibly be giving it more significance than Jesus intended. It is quite possible that he was simply admonishing the centurions in the same way that we would say "God forgive you!" to someone who hurt us, and not intending it as a teaching for us at all. He could also have simply meant that they did not know they were killing the Son of God, and so could not understand the vast implications of their deed.

Although it's arguable that Jesus asked Father God to forgive those who crucified him, it is interesting to note that all the gospels agree on one point- he *didn't* say to them, "*I* forgive you." Although he could have if he wanted to, *Jesus did not offer his own forgiveness to those who abused him.* Our Lord did not use this as a golden opportunity to set an example for us of forgiving the unrepentant. Even in his last words, Jesus did not give us any reason to think that *he* had forgiven his murderers.

The question of whether or not Father God actually forgave those who killed Jesus despite their unrepentance *is left unanswered and remains unknown to this day. There is absolutely no indication that God did indeed forgive them, and no reason to assume that he did.* This would be nothing but pure unsubstantiated speculation.

Another interesting point is that three of the gospels make mention of the centurion's and others' reactions when Jesus died, the rocks moved, and the curtain of the temple was torn in two:

NOW WHEN THE CENTURION, AND THEY THAT WERE WITH HIM, WATCHING JESUS, SAW THE EARTHQUAKE, AND THOSE THINGS THAT WERE DONE, THEY FEARED GREATLY, SAYING, TRULY THIS WAS THE SON OF GOD.... Matthew 27:54 KJV.

AND JESUS CRIED WITH A LOUD VOICE, AND GAVE UP THE GHOST. AND THE VAIL OF THE TEMPLE WAS RENT IN TWAIN FROM THE TOP TO THE BOTTOM. AND WHEN THE CENTURION, WHICH STOOD OVER AGAINST HIM, SAW THAT HE SO CRIED OUT, AND GAVE UP THE GHOST, HE SAID, TRULY THIS MAN WAS THE SON OF GOD....Mark 15:37-39 KJV.

IT WAS NOW ABOUT THE SIXTH HOUR, AND DARKNESS CAME OVER THE WHOLE LAND UNTIL THE NINTH HOUR, FOR THE SUN STOPPED SHINING. AND THE CURTAIN OF THE TEMPLE WAS TORN IN TWO. JESUS

CALLED OUT WITH A LOUD VOICE, "FATHER, INTO YOUR HANDS I COMMIT MY SPIRIT." WHEN HE HAD SAID THIS, HE BREATHED HIS LAST. THE CENTURION, SEEING WHAT HAD HAPPENED, PRAISED GOD AND SAID, "SURELY THIS WAS A RIGHTEOUS MAN." WHEN ALL THE PEOPLE WHO HAD GATHERED TO WITNESS THIS SIGHT SAW WHAT TOOK PLACE, THEY BEAT THEIR BREASTS AND WENT AWAY...Luke 23:44-48 NIV.

Could we not take this to mean that at least one, if not some or even all, of those who killed Jesus, realized what they had done and did in fact repent? It certainly seems as if at least this one man, the centurion, did feel regret and remorse- or even horror that he had helped to kill the Son of God. If, in fact, any of those who killed Jesus praised God as Luke said and repented, then we know they were forgiven, *because they repented!*

However, for the most part I find I can only have discussions like this with other believers. In my opinion, most of this is much too deep to get into with non-believers or abusers and their Flying Monkeys, who challenge that repentance is a require- ment for forgiveness. They're not looking for a complicated Bible study. They're just looking for an excuse to be entitled to forgive- ness without changing their ways. Those whose eyes are veiled have no understanding and will debate everything in the Bible that is not completely spelled out so that they can pick it apart, twist it, and find flaws.

Rather than get into a long-drawn-out argument, I prefer to simplify it for them. Let's assume that Jesus did say it. In that case, what he said was, "Father, forgive them; *for they know not what they do.*" That is the key to this verse. He is saying that God does not hold you responsible for sinning if you don't understand what you're doing or know that it's wrong. Just like a child who has not yet reached the age of reason, you are not considered respon- sible for your actions if you lack the capacity to understand them.

I'm sure all of us have at one time or another overlooked an offense and forgiven- because we knew that the person who hurt us really didn't know what he was doing, made a genuine mistake, is not normally malicious, didn't mean any harm or didn't anticipate the consequences his actions might have.

However, no one who has been in an abusive relationship can say that an abuser doesn't know what he's doing. *In fact, abusers know exactly what they're doing.* Abuse is intentional, deliberate, ongoing, and often planned out in detail and in advance. It is also repetitive in nature, and the abuser keeps on doing it because it works for him. Abusers are also able to control their behavior just fine, and we've all seen them do it when there are witnesses they wish to impress, or when controlling it will benefit them in some other way. Deliberate malice and intentional disregard for the feelings and welfare of others might be hard for some of us to absorb, but these are the hallmarks of narcissists, bullies, abusers and psychopaths.

Even if we wanted to give an abuser/narcissist the benefit of the doubt and assume that he really doesn't have enough sense to understand that his behavior is wrong or to realize the harm it causes, once we confront him and make this clear, *now* what's the excuse? And what is his usual reaction? As we all know, it is never a sincere apology and a change in behavior. Instead, it's more abuse in the form of denial, lies, blame, rage, etc., and the behavior we originally rebuked continues or even escalates. This pretty much removes all doubt that the abuser "doesn't know what he's doing." Because now he's been *told* what he's doing, and he's choosing to do it anyway.

In this particular verse, Jesus does not speak in generalities but rather is quite specific. He asked God to forgive those who did not have the ability to know what they were doing and to understand that it was wrong. But abusers don't have that excuse. They are not innocent or naïve, and therefore don't qualify for forgiveness on the basis of not knowing what they are doing. *If you have any doubts as to whether your abuser has the capacity to understand that her behavior is wrong, just threaten to tell other people what she did and watch her go ballistic when she thinks you're going to expose her.* If she really believed that she didn't do anything wrong, then she'd have no problem with the whole world knowing what she did. In fact, she'd be proud of herself.

For someone who has the ability to know what he's doing and that his behavior is unacceptable, repentance is still the biblical requirement for forgiveness. As for those who killed Jesus and did not repent, the Bible never says that they were forgiven despite their unrepentance. So I stand by my statement that there is not one instance of forgiveness without repentance in the Bible.

This is a typical example of one of the most common abusive defense tactics- abusers jumping all over what they think is an opportunity to use the Bible for their own benefit. They twist what it says, read into what it doesn't say, add their own thoughts, interpret it to their advantage, take it out of context, make assumptions, and jump to conclusions that are not at all supported in Luke's gospel. And when quoting a scripture to use against us, they also conveniently manage to omit half, or even more than half, of the scripture if it does not support their case. However, if we read this verse exactly as Jesus supposedly said it, it does not contradict our position that God requires repentance before forgiveness. Abusers who try to misrepresent the Bible for their own purposes don't like to be corrected. But if they're going to attempt to use the Word of God for evil, then it is our responsibility to our Lord to not allow it.

Sisters and Brothers, never forget that the father of lies, disorder and confusion is Satan, and his children will try their best to lie and confuse us so that they can continue their evil unchecked. But whenever there seems to be a contradiction or confusion about something in the Bible, it helps to remind ourselves that God *never said* anything, and *never will say* anything, that would make it easier for an abuser to keep on abusing, or a sinner to keep on sinning. There is nothing in the Word of God that facilitates or supports evil in any way.

I pray that this explanation will be useful to you when you are confronted by an abuser or a holier-than-thou Flying Monkey who uses this misleading argument. Praise the Lord and thank you Holy Spirit for your gift of understanding.

WHY IS MY LANGUAGE NOT CLEAR TO YOU? BECAUSE YOU ARE UNABLE TO HEAR WHAT I SAY. YOU BELONG TO YOUR FATHER, THE DEVIL, AND YOU WANT TO CARRY OUT YOUR FATHER'S DESIRE. HE WAS A MURDERER FROM THE BEGINNING, NOT HOLDING TO THE TRUTH, FOR THERE IS NO TRUTH IN HIM. WHEN HE LIES, HE SPEAKS HIS NATIVE LANGUAGE, FOR HE IS A LIAR AND THE FATHER OF LIES. YET BECAUSE I TELL THE TRUTH, YOU DO NOT BELIEVE ME! CAN ANY OF YOU PROVE ME GUILTY OF SIN? IF I AM TELLING THE TRUTH, WHY DON'T YOU BELIEVE ME? HE WHO BELONGS TO GOD HEARS WHAT GOD SAYS. THE REASON YOU DO NOT HEAR IS THAT YOU DO NOT BELONG TO GOD....John 8:43-47 NIV.

HE REPLIED, "THE KNOWLEDGE OF THE SECRETS OF THE KINGDOM OF HEAVEN HAS BEEN GIVEN TO YOU, BUT NOT TO THEM. WHOEVER HAS WILL BE GIVEN MORE, AND HE WILL HAVE AN ABUNDANCE. WHOEVER DOES NOT HAVE, EVEN WHAT HE HAS WILL BE TAKEN FROM HIM. THIS IS WHY I SPEAK TO THEM IN PARABLES: "THOUGH SEEING, THEY DO NOT SEE; THOUGH HEARING, THEY DO NOT HEAR OR UNDERSTAND. IN THEM IS FULFILLED THE PROPHECY OF ISAIAH: 'YOU WILL BE EVER HEARING BUT NEVER UNDERSTANDING; YOU WILL BE EVER SEEING BUT

NEVER PERCEIVING. FOR THIS PEOPLE'S HEART HAS BECOME CALLOUSED; THEY HARDLY HEAR WITH THEIR EARS, AND THEY HAVE CLOSED THEIR EYES. OTHERWISE THEY MIGHT SEE WITH THEIR EYES, HEAR WITH THEIR EARS, UNDERSTAND WITH THEIR HEARTS AND TURN, AND I WOULD HEAL THEM." BUT BLESSED ARE YOUR EYES BECAUSE THEY SEE, AND YOUR EARS BECAUSE THEY HEAR. FOR I TELL YOU THE TRUTH, MANY PROPHETS AND RIGHTEOUS MEN LONGED TO SEE WHAT YOU SEE BUT DID NOT SEE IT, AND TO HEAR WHAT YOU HEAR BUT DID NOT HEAR IT....Matthew 13:11-17 NIV.

Chapter 9

How Can I Tell if the Person who Hurt Me is Really a "Brother" in Christ?

YE SHALL KNOW THEM BY THEIR FRUITS. *DO MEN GATHER GRAPES OF THORNS, OR FIGS OF THISTLES? EVEN SO EVERY GOOD TREE BRINGETH FORTH GOOD FRUIT; BUT A CORRUPT TREE BRINGETH FORTH EVIL FRUIT. A GOOD TREE CANNOT BRING FORTH EVIL FRUIT, NEITHER CAN A CORRUPT TREE BRING FORTH GOOD FRUIT. EVERY TREE THAT BRINGETH NOT FORTH GOOD FRUIT IS HEWN DOWN, AND CAST INTO THE FIRE. WHEREFORE BY THEIR FRUITS YE SHALL KNOW THEM.* **NOT EVERY ONE THAT SAITH UNTO ME, LORD, LORD, SHALL ENTER INTO THE KINGDOM OF HEAVEN;** *BUT HE THAT DOETH THE WILL OF MY FATHER WHICH IS IN HEAVEN. MANY WILL SAY TO ME IN THAT DAY, LORD, LORD, HAVE WE NOT PROPHESIED IN THY NAME? AND IN THY NAME HAVE CAST OUT DEVILS? AND IN THY NAME DONE MANY WONDERFUL WORKS? AND THEN I WILL PROFESS UNTO THEM, I NEVER KNEW YOU: DEPART FROM ME, YE THAT WORK INIQUITY...Matthew 7:16-23 KJV.*

NO ONE WHO IS BORN OF GOD WILL CONTINUE TO SIN, BECAUSE GOD'S SEED REMAINS IN HIM; HE CANNOT GO ON SINNING, BECAUSE HE HAS BEEN BORN OF GOD. THIS IS HOW WE KNOW WHO THE CHILDREN OF GOD ARE AND WHO THE CHILDREN OF THE DEVIL ARE: ANYONE WHO DOES NOT DO WHAT IS RIGHT IS NOT A CHILD OF GOD, NOR IS ANYONE WHO DOES NOT LOVE HIS BROTHER...1John 3:9-10 NIV.

So how can we tell if we're dealing with a true "brother" or "sister" in Christ, or a phony one? The Bible pretty much spells it out for us. In Matthew, Jesus teaches us to look at a person's fruit, which is what he produces in his life. And in 1 John, we are clearly told that a real child of God will not continue to sin and anyone who does not do what is right is not a child of God. Take time to observe and listen, keeping these teachings in mind, and pray to the Holy Ghost for the gift of the discernment of spirits.

Because there can be no such thing as a "Christian" abuser, a "Christian" back-stabber, a "Christian" gossip, a "Christian" liar, a "Christian" pedophile, a "Christian" thief, a "Christian" manipulator, etc., etc., it does not mean that those who do these things must actually be innocent and not really behaving in these ways, and we must have "misunderstood" in some way. What it means is that they are not really Christian.

Another major difference between real Christians and pretend Christians is that *an unrighteous person will not repent* when he is rebuked, but a *real* Christian will learn from rebuke and change his ways (Proverbs 9:8-9; 12:1; 12:15; 15:31; 29:1). This will confirm your discernment of a fake "Christian." The Bible refers to those who refuse to make amends for what they have done as "fools" who do not have goodwill for others:

FOOLS MOCK AT MAKING AMENDS FOR SIN, BUT GOODWILL IS FOUND AMONG THE UPRIGHT.... Proverbs 14:9 NIV.

This is how we are instructed to deal with mockers:

DRIVE OUT THE MOCKER, AND OUT GOES STRIFE; QUARRELS AND INSULTS ARE ENDED....Proverbs 22:10 NIV.

Godly people accept rebuke, learn from it, make amends and change their ways. *Real* Christians, who have goodwill and love in their hearts and truly don't mean to offend, have no problem doing this, and so could rightfully expect to be forgiven. They do not make excuses for offensive behavior. They apologize and correct it. This is what the Bible tells us to do when we have hurt someone:

*IF YOU HAVE BEEN TRAPPED BY WHAT YOU SAID, ENSNARED BY THE WORDS OF YOUR MOUTH, THEN DO THIS, MY SON, TO FREE YOURSELF, SINCE YOU HAVE FALLEN INTO YOUR NEIGHBOR'S HANDS: **GO AND HUMBLE YOURSELF;** PRESS YOUR PLEA WITH YOUR NEIGHBOR! ALLOW NO SLEEP TO YOUR EYES, NO SLUMBER TO YOUR EYELIDS. FREE YOURSELF, LIKE A GAZELLE FROM THE HAND OF THE HUNTER, LIKE A BIRD FROM THE SNARE OF THE FOWLER....Proverbs 6: 2-5 NIV.*

Ungodly people, on the other hand, show no remorse and have a variety of defenses for justifying behavior which causes pain for others. When rebuked, they will deny, make excuses, pout, become defensive, lay on a guilt trip, display unrighteous anger, minimize their offense, claim it was all a "misunderstanding," turn it around and pretend to be the one who was offended, or display any of the dozens of other inappropriate responses which abusers have in their arsenal. They will make no effort to change their hurtful behavior. They will blame the victim, or someone or something else, for what they do or say. They will even blame the devil! What they are overlooking here is that they were given free will:

SUBMIT YOURSELVES THEREFORE TO GOD. RESIST THE DEVIL, AND HE WILL FLEE FROM YOU...James 4:7 KJV.

No one can say, "The devil made me do it." *The devil cannot make you do anything.* All he can do is tempt you. You make the choice whether to listen to him or not. People who do everything *but* take responsibility for the damage they have caused, admit that their victim was right to be hurt or offended, and do their best to make amends *are not Christians-* even if they claim to be. They are narcissists, abusers, sociopaths, and/or psychopaths. These are fake Christians, the wolves in sheep's clothing, false teachers, false prophets, reprobates and children of Satan we are warned about in the Bible.

The unrighteous are not humble, like true Christians are. They are very prideful. They do not want to admit they were *wrong* and that they should not have done whatever it was they did. They will do everything to avoid committing to a permanent change in their behavior, as if it is not really under their control. They will say things like, "We were *both* wrong," or, "We have *both* hurt each other," *when in reality the victim did nothing wrong at all.* They may or may not grudgingly apologize, but they rarely *change* their ways. Again, in the Bible those who do not listen to rebuke are referred to as "fools." They are not called "righteous", "godly," or anything else that sounds the least bit "Christian-like," and we are instructed not to waste our time trying to reason with them. We are admonished to stay away from fools who will not listen to rebuke, and told not even to speak to them:

DO NOT SPEAK TO A FOOL, FOR HE WILL SCORN THE WISDOM OF YOUR WORDS....Proverbs 23:9 NIV.

I think it is also relevant here to understand that nowhere in the Bible are we instructed to "analyze" or "try to be understanding" of someone whose actions are cruel, unloving or abusive. There is no psychology in the Bible. Scripture very simply teaches us to rebuke if we have been offended, forgive if there is repentance, and have nothing further to do with one who does not repent or listen to rebuke. An abuser's list of excuses (unhappy childhood, stress, trauma, drugs, alcohol, personality disorders, emotional problems, etc.) are meaningless and do not make his actions or words any less destructive. No one has the right to inflict their issues on anyone else. The "reasons" for unacceptable behavior don't matter. Christians are to take a stand against wickedness and all forms of evil, regardless of the "justification" for it.

If it were true that fake Christian abusers and abuse-defenders were actually real brothers and sisters in the faith, even *more* would be expected of them, not less. As we have seen, there are far *more* scriptures referring to the rebuke of a "brother" than there are about rebuking a non-believer. Children of God are held to an even *higher* standard than children of the world, and certainly higher than children of the devil. A child of God is supposed to be setting a good example for others. He is not supposed to behave just as badly as, or even worse than, everybody else.

In Galatians chapter 5, Christians are instructed to expel an immoral brother from among them *and not associate with him.* Paul specifically tells us not to bother judging those *outside* the church, but to judge those *inside* the church:

I HAVE WRITTEN YOU IN MY LETTER NOT TO ASSOCIATE WITH SEXUALLY IMMORAL PEOPLE-NOT AT ALL MEANING THE PEOPLE OF THIS WORLD WHO

ARE IMMORAL, OR THE GREEDY AND SWINDLERS, OR IDOLATERS. IN THAT CASE YOU WOULD HAVE TO LEAVE THIS WORLD. BUT NOW I AM WRITING YOU THAT **YOU MUST NOT ASSOCIATE WITH ANYONE WHO CALLS HIMSELF A BROTHER** *BUT IS SEXUALLY IMMORAL OR GREEDY, AN IDOLATER OR A SLANDERER, A DRUNKARD OR A SWINDLER. WITH SUCH A MAN DO NOT EVEN EAT. WHAT BUSINESS IS IT OF MINE TO JUDGE THOSE OUTSIDE THE CHURCH? ARE YOU NOT TO JUDGE THOSE INSIDE? GOD WILL JUDGE THOSE OUTSIDE. EXPEL THE WICKED MAN FROM AMONG YOU.....1 Corinthians 5:9-13 NIV.*

In Deuteronomy, the children of God are told, *"YOU MUST PURGE THE EVIL FROM AMONG YOU"* six separate times (Deuteronomy 17:7; 19:19; 21:21; 22:21; 22:23; and 24:7 {NIV}). These are just some of the scriptures instructing us to hold fellow children of God accountable for their behavior.

What about those phony "Christians" who claim Jesus as their Savior, but keep behaving wickedly? Paul teaches us that they cannot be renewed into repentance again, because by going back to their evil after knowing Jesus, they have crucified the Son of God once more and put him to shame. Because they do not bear the fruit of repentance and righteousness, but thorns and briers, they are rejected by God and cursed, and their end is to be burned:

AND THIS WILL WE DO, IF GOD PERMIT. **FOR IT IS IMPOSSIBLE FOR THOSE WHO WERE ONCE ENLIGHTENED, AND HAVE TASTED OF THE HEAVENLY GIFT, AND WERE MADE PARTAKERS OF THE HOLY GHOST, AND HAVE TASTED THE GOOD WORD OF GOD, AND THE POWERS OF THE WORLD TO COME, IF THEY SHALL FALL AWAY, TO RENEW**

THEM AGAIN UNTO REPENTANCE; SEEING THEY CRUCIFY TO THEMSELVES THE SON OF GOD AFRESH, AND PUT HIM TO AN OPEN SHAME. FOR THE EARTH WHICH DRINKETH IN THE RAIN THAT COMETH OFT UPON IT, AND BRINGETH FORTH HERBS MEET FOR THEM BY WHOM IT IS DRESSED, RECEIVETH BLESSING FROM GOD: BUT THAT WHICH BEARETH THORNS AND BRIERS IS REJECTED, AND IS NIGH UNTO CURSING; WHOSE END IS TO BE BURNED....Hebrews 6:3-8 KJV.

Jesus teaches us that we will know them by their fruit. Think back and be honest about the "fruit" the one who offended you produces in her life. Look beneath the surface, ignore the "nice" façade and the good impression she tries to make. Pray for discernment and the Holy Ghost will give it to you. Listen to his still small voice. By his grace you will see clearly and be able to discern a real Christian from a phony one. Thank you Lord.

Chapter 10

Rebuking

*THEM THAT SIN **REBUKE BEFORE ALL**, THAT OTHERS ALSO MAY FEAR.....1 Timothy 5:20 KJV.*

*WHEN I SAY UNTO THE WICKED, O WICKED MAN, THOU SHALT SURELY DIE; IF THOU DOST NOT SPEAK TO **WARN THE WICKED** FROM HIS WAY, THAT WICKED MAN SHALL DIE IN HIS INIQUITY; BUT HIS BLOOD WILL I REQUIRE AT THINE HAND. NEVERTHELESS, IF THOU WARN THE WICKED OF HIS WAY TO TURN FROM IT; IF HE DO NOT TURN FROM HIS WAY, HE SHALL DIE IN HIS INIQUITY; BUT THOU HAST DELIVERED THY SOUL.... Ezekiel 33: 8-9 KJV.*

I wonder where folks get the idea that Christians have to be meek and mild, silently enduring mistreatment, tolerating anything anybody else does, and timidly standing by while abusers trample all over them and other innocent victims. Since when is it a sin to speak out against evil? Since when is it virtuous to look the other way when someone (including ourselves) is being bullied or abused? This is what our abusers want us to believe, and they just love throwing it in our faces anytime we protest their behavior. They provoke us to anger, they cause untold pain and suffering, and then when we finally speak up, they smugly inform us that *we're* the ones not acting like "good Christians."

This is hogwash. Abusers would just love for us to back off and be quiet while they do anything they want and get away with murder. Satan will always try to use our righteousness against us, to get us to question our faith and to separate us from God. This is just another one of his tricks. What kind of awesome, wonderful, all-good God would our Father be if he actually wanted us to allow wickedness to operate unchecked in our families and in our lives? This concept is another preposterous figment of our abuser's and their Monkey's imaginations, and contradicts the perfect goodness of the Lord. Our God is all good, and the devil is all bad. They are diametrically opposed for all eternity. God instructs his saints to take a stand against evil and fight the good fight, not to keep silent and hide in the closet. It is God's plan that good will triumph over evil. We are the Army of God. We must put on the full armor of God and stand against Satan and his army. That is our assignment, and our destiny as a child of God.

> **WARN** *A DIVISIVE PERSON ONCE, THEN* **WARN** *HIM A SECOND TIME. AFTER THAT,* **HAVE NOTHING TO DO WITH HIM**. *YOU MAY BE SURE THAT SUCH A MAN IS WARPED AND SINFUL; HE IS SELF-CONDEMNED.....* Titus 3:10-11 NIV.

> *ANSWER A FOOL ACCORDING TO HIS FOLLY, LEST HE BE WISE IN HIS OWN EYES....Proverbs 26:5 NKJV.*

> *THEN WILL I TEACH TRANSGRESSORS THY WAYS; AND SINNERS SHALL BE CONVERTED UNTO THEE....Psalm 51:13 KJV.*

BEHOLD, I GIVE UNTO YOU POWER TO TREAD ON SERPENTS AND SCORPIONS, AND OVER ALL THE POWER OF THE ENEMY: AND NOTHING SHALL BY ANY MEANS HURT YOU. NOTWITHSTANDING IN THIS REJOICE NOT, THAT THE SPIRITS ARE SUBJECT UNTO YOU; BUT RATHER REJOICE, BECAUSE YOUR NAMES ARE WRITTEN IN HEAVEN....Luke 10:19-20 KJV.

Chapter 11

Rebuke is for Their Own Good

SPEAK UP *FOR THOSE WHO CANNOT SPEAK FOR THEMSELVES, FOR THE RIGHTS OF ALL WHO ARE DESTITUTE. SPEAK UP AND JUDGE FAIRLY: DEFEND THE RIGHTS OF THE POOR AND NEEDY...Proverbs 31:8-9 NIV.*

DO NOT HATE YOUR BROTHER IN YOUR HEART. **REBUKE YOUR NEIGHBOR FRANKLY** *SO YOU WILL NOT SHARE IN HIS GUILT...Leviticus 19:17 NIV.*

THOSE WHO SIN ARE TO BE **REBUKED PUBLICLY**, *SO THAT THE OTHERS MAY TAKE WARNING...1 Timothy 5:20 NIV.*

MEN OF PERVERSE HEART SHALL BE FAR FROM ME: I WILL HAVE NOTHING TO DO WITH EVIL. *WHOEVER SLANDERS HIS NEIGHBOR IN SECRET, HIM WILL I PUT TO SILENCE; WHOEVER HAS HAUGHTY EYES AND A PROUD HEART, HIM WILL I NOT ENDURE....NO ONE WHO PRACTICES DECEIT WILL DWELL IN MY HOUSE; NO ONE*

*WHO SPEAKS FALSELY WILL STAND IN MY PRESENCE. EVERY MORNING I WILL PUT TO SILENCE ALL THE WICKED IN THE LAND: **I WILL CUT OFF EVERY EVILDOER** FROM THE CITY OF THE LORD…..Psalm 101:4-5, 7-8 NIV.*

REBUKE: To express severe disapproval or sharp criticism, to reprimand severely.

*"SON OF MAN, I HAVE MADE YOU A WATCHMAN FOR THE HOUSE OF ISRAEL: SO HEAR THE WORD I SPEAK AND **GIVE THEM WARNING FROM ME**. WHEN I SAY TO THE WICKED, 'O WICKED MAN, YOU WILL SURELY DIE,' AND YOU DO NOT SPEAK OUT TO DISSUADE HIM FROM HIS WAYS, THAT WICKED MAN WILL DIE FOR HIS SIN, AND I WILL HOLD YOU ACCOUNTABLE FOR HIS BLOOD. BUT IF YOU DO WARN THE WICKED MAN TO TURN FROM HIS WAYS AND HE DOES NOT DO SO, HE WILL DIE FOR HIS SIN, BUT YOU WILL HAVE SAVED YOURSELF….. SAY TO THEM, "AS SURELY AS I LIVE, DECLARES THE SOVEREIGN LORD, I TAKE NO PLEASURE IN THE DEATH OF THE WICKED, BUT RATHER THAT THEY TURN FROM THEIR WAYS AND LIVE. TURN! TURN FROM YOUR EVIL WAYS! WHY WILL YOU DIE, O HOUSE OF ISRAEL?"….Ezekiel 33:7-9, 11 NIV.*

Well, the Lord can't make it any clearer than that! If ever we had any doubts that God wants us to take a stand and speak up against evil, this passage should erase them. *The Lord tells us that **we sin when we remain silent** about wickedness.* God tells us that we are doing an offender a *favor* by rebuking her. Offenders themselves may not see it that way- but, quite frankly, their opinions don't matter.

Although we hesitate, and sometimes don't know quite what to say, rebuking a wrongdoer isn't really all that complicated. Rebuking is simply making a statement directly to the offender. It is saying to him, "What you're doing is wrong, and I don't condone it," or, "What you did was wrong, and you need to be accountable for it."

Rebuke is not condemnation, rebuke is *correction*. It is teaching, pointing someone in the right direction, showing him- by our disapproval of his behavior- what is appropriate and acceptable, and what is not. When we rebuke, we are warning a wicked person. We are giving him a chance to change his ways and save his soul. God *wants* him to turn from evil and be saved. He does not want anyone to continue sinning and be condemned to hell. Therefore, he assigns us a divine mandate to *rebuke* when we see evil being committed.

So, why are we so reluctant to speak up? Maybe we never thought of it as being on a Mission from God before, but that's what it is. Our mission is to turn as many souls to the Lord and away from the devil as possible. And rebuke is the God-given tool by which we will do that.

*AND NOT BY HIS COMING ONLY, BUT BY THE CONSOLATION WHEREWITH HE WAS COMFORTED IN YOU, WHEN HE TOLD US YOUR EARNEST DESIRE, YOUR MOURNING, YOUR FERVENT MIND TOWARD ME: SO THAT I REJOICED THE MORE. FOR THOUGH I MADE YOU SORRY WITH A LETTER, I DO NOT REPENT, THOUGH I DID REPENT: FOR I PERCEIVE THAT THE SAME EPISTLE HATH MADE YOU SORRY, THOUGH IT WERE BUT FOR A SEASON. **NOW I REJOICE, NOT THAT YE WERE MADE SORRY, BUT THAT YE SORROWED TO REPENTANCE**: FOR YE WERE MADE SORRY AFTER A GODLY MANNER, THAT YE MIGHT RECEIVE DAMAGE*

BY US IN NOTHING. **FOR GODLY SORROW WORKETH REPENTANCE TO SALVATION NOT TO BE REPENTED OF: BUT THE SORROW OF THE WORLD WORKETH DEATH**....*2Corinthians 7:7-10 KJV.*

In the above passage, notice that Paul does not apologize for rebuking the Corinthians and "hurting their feelings." He says that he is glad that he rebuked them and made them sorry for what they did, because it resulted in their godly repentance. Here Paul also describes godly repentance, and teaches us that worldly (self-serving) repentance is not acceptable. Godly remorse is not concerned with benefiting the wicked one in some way. Remorse given just to end the argument, get back in the victim's good graces, stay out of jail, not "look bad," or otherwise help the offender is not true repentance; it is "the sorrow of the world" Paul speaks of, which worketh death. True repentance is concerned only with making the victim feel better and making her whole.

Unfortunately, most wicked people are fools who will not turn from their sin. However, the Bible tells us that righteous people *will* appreciate our rebuke and heed us. By rebuking, we can help good people to see the error of their ways, avoid destructive or hurtful behavior, grow in the Lord, and walk more closely with God:

DO NOT CORRECT A SCOFFER, LEST HE HATE YOU: REBUKE A WISE MAN, AND HE WILL LOVE YOU; GIVE INSTRUCTION TO A WISE MAN, AND HE WILL BE STILL WISER; TEACH A JUST MAN, AND HE WILL INCREASE IN LEARNING.....Proverbs 9:8-9 NKJV.

HE THAT REBUKETH A MAN, AFTERWARDS SHALL FIND MORE FAVOUR THAN HE THAT FLATTERETH WITH THE TONGUE...Proverbs 28:23 KJV.

FLOG A MOCKER, AND THE SIMPLE WILL LEARN PRUDENCE: REBUKE A DISCERNING MAN, AND HE WILL GAIN KNOWLEDGE ...Proverbs 19:25 NIV.

THE FEAR OF THE LORD IS THE BEGINNING OF KNOWLEDGE: BUT FOOLS DESPISE WISDOM AND INSTRUCTION.....Proverbs 1:7 KJV.

These verses are the biblical version of "You can't win them all," but we're still supposed to try. Those who can be saved, will be saved. And those who can't be saved, by their own choice, won't be.

Rebuking is different from setting limits or boundaries. We set boundaries on *future* behavior, but we rebuke *past or present* behavior. We usually rebuke *ongoing* behavior, but we might also rebuke a one-time offense which caused pain for us or for someone else.

Many times rebuking goes hand in hand with setting boundaries. After we have rebuked an offender for something he has already done or is doing on an ongoing basis, then we set limits on what we will tolerate from that point on. Rebuke is the first step in letting someone know that his actions or words are unacceptable and will not be condoned. Boundaries are the next step, to make clear what is or is not acceptable in the future.

Rebuking can be described as "speaking the truth in love." Both truth and love are important. Being loving does not mean that we cover up, whitewash, avoid, deny, or don't speak the truth. *And telling it like it is does not mean that we are unloving,* although offenders will often try to make us feel guilty for doing so. Speaking the truth is stating, quite simply and clearly, what the offender has done, that his behavior is unacceptable, and what the results of his actions or words were, including the pain inflicted on someone else. *Since we did not cause the pain,* simply describing it and stating the facts is nothing for *us* to feel guilty about.

Speaking the truth plainly does not mean that we cannot do it with love. We need to at least start out with a spirit of reconciliation and the hope of resolving the problem. Whether this is possible or not is not solely up to us, but will depend upon the offender's reaction to our rebuke. Our only obligation is to live in peace with others *as far as it depends on us* (Romans 12:18). However, God recognizes that it is not always possible to live in peace with everybody, *because it does not always depend on us*, and we need to realize this, too. We are not responsible for an abuser's negative reaction to our rebuke, or for his refusal to listen to us. We are only responsible for rebuking him in the first place. If he refuses to repent and change his ways, then our responsibility ends, and we are released from any further obligation to forgive him or to continue the relationship under those circumstances. In fact, at this point, the Bible tells us to have nothing more to do with him (Titus 3:10-11; Matthew 18:15-17; Mark 6:11; 2 Corinthians 6:14-18; 2 Timothy 3:2-5; Matthew 7:6; 1 Corinthians 15:33; 1 Corinthians 5:2, 4-5, 11, 13; Proverbs 22:10, 24-25; Deuteronomy 17:7).

Rebuking with love does not mean that we must be passive, wishy-washy, reluctant, or even calm when we rebuke. How we approach having to rebuke an offender has more to do with *his* nature than with ours. We need to adapt our approach to the offender's personality and character.

Jesus tailored the forcefulness of his rebukes to the personalities of those whom he was rebuking. When he met the Samaritan woman at the well, he stated the facts of her sin gently but firmly:

"I HAVE NO HUSBAND," SHE REPLIED. JESUS SAID TO HER, "YOU ARE RIGHT WHEN YOU SAY YOU HAVE NO HUSBAND. THE FACT IS, YOU HAVE HAD FIVE HUSBANDS, AND THE MAN YOU NOW HAVE IS NOT

YOUR HUSBAND. WHAT YOU HAVE JUST SAID IS QUITE TRUE"…..John 4:16-17 NIV.

Jesus knew the hearts of his disciples, and rebuked them gently as well:

AND THOMAS ANSWERED AND SAID UNTO HIM, MY LORD AND MY GOD. JESUS SAITH UNTO HIM, THOMAS, BECAUSE THOU HAST SEEN ME, THOU HAST BELIEVED: BLESSED ARE THEY THAT HAVE NOT SEEN, AND YET HAVE BELIEVED….John 20:28-29 KJV.

AND THE LORD SAID, "SIMON, SIMON! INDEED, SATAN HAS ASKED FOR YOU, THAT HE MAY SIFT YOU AS WHEAT. BUT I HAVE PRAYED FOR YOU, THAT YOUR FAITH MAY NOT FAIL; AND WHEN YOU HAVE RETURNED TO ME, STRENGTHEN YOUR BRETHREN." BUT HE SAID TO HIM, "LORD, I AM READY TO GO WITH YOU, BOTH TO PRISON AND TO DEATH." THEN HE SAID, "I TELL YOU, PETER, THE ROOSTER SHALL NOT CROW THIS DAY BEFORE YOU WILL DENY THREE TIMES THAT YOU KNOW ME."….Luke 22:31-34 NKJV.

With some people, we will need to take a mild but firm approach, because anything stronger will overwhelm or devastate them. These people are usually not chronic abusers, as chronic abusers typically have much thicker skins. Perhaps they are simply thoughtless or inconsiderate. Blasting them with both barrels would be very hurtful and counterproductive. We may wind up doing far more damage to the relationship than the original offense did. Approaching them in a calm, laid-back manner and in a spirit of cooperation will give us the best chance for restoring the relationship to one that we can all be happy with. This is the best possible scenario, where everyone involved acts out of love, so that each person's feelings can be validated, and the hurtful behavior will stop.

Unfortunately, at the other extreme is the malicious abuser-the one whose behavior is outrageous and destructive, the one who betrayed you, the one with no remorse, the ruthless psychopath who couldn't care less about anybody but herself, the one who makes your life, and probably everyone else's lives, a living hell. This is not the type of offender you pussyfoot around. You are never going to get anywhere with such a person by being gentle and low-key. You will probably have no choice but to raise your voice just to be heard. This is the time to break out the big guns, make sure your rebuke is very strong, and make your disapproval of her behavior loud and clear. Allow yourself some righteous anger, and allow that anger to show.

Now, none of this means that you don't love your friend or relative. Indeed, you are putting yourself through all this turmoil just to make your relationship better, when you could just end it and change your phone number! What it does mean is simply that your friend or relative's stubborn, "stiff-necked" and unloving nature makes it necessary for your rebuke to be powerful. Anything less, and this abuser will just steamroll right over you-and nothing will be accomplished at all.

Again, we turn to Jesus' example to teach us how to forcefully rebuke a prideful, stubborn, or seriously abusive person when the situation calls for it. His rebukes of the Pharisees illustrate for us how to confront those who will not turn from their evil:

"WOE TO YOU, TEACHERS OF THE LAW AND PHARISEES, YOU HYPOCRITES! YOU TRAVEL OVER LAND AND SEA TO WIN A SINGLE CONVERT, AND WHEN HE BECOMES ONE, YOU MAKE HIM TWICE AS MUCH A SON OF HELL AS YOU ARE."...Matthew 23:15 NIV.

WOE UNTO YOU, SCRIBES AND PHARISEES, HYPOCRITES! FOR YE ARE LIKE UNTO WHITED SEPULCHRES, WHICH INDEED APPEAR BEAUTIFUL OUTWARD, BUT ARE WITHIN FULL OF DEAD MEN'S BONES, AND OF ALL UNCLEANNESS. EVEN SO YE ALSO OUTWARDLY APPEAR RIGHTEOUS UNTO MEN, BUT WITHIN YE ARE FULL OF HYPOCRISY AND INIQUITY....Matthew 23:27-28 KJV.

"YOU SNAKES! YOU BROOD OF VIPERS! HOW WILL YOU ESCAPE BEING CONDEMNED TO HELL? THEREFORE I AM SENDING YOU PROPHETS AND WISE MEN AND TEACHERS. SOME OF THEM YOU WILL KILL AND CRUCIFY; OTHERS YOU WILL FLOG IN YOUR SYNAGOGUES AND PURSUE FROM TOWN TO TOWN. AND SO UPON YOU WILL COME ALL THE RIGHTEOUS BLOOD THAT HAS BEEN SHED ON EARTH, FROM THE BLOOD OF THE RIGHTEOUS ABEL TO THE BLOOD OF ZECHARIAH SON OF BEREKIAH, WHOM YOU MURDERED BETWEEN THE TEMPLE AND THE ALTAR"....Matthew 23:33-35 NIV.

I have to chuckle when I imagine one of us having the courage to call even downright wicked people "sons of hell", "snakes," or a "brood of vipers." It seems that we try so hard to voice our complaints about someone's mistreatment in a "nice" way, even though that rarely gets us anywhere with true abusers. One way of looking at it is that with some people, you might as well prepare yourself, because there is no way, no matter how nicely you try to approach them, that you are not going to wind up in a big fight anyhow. This is *their* doing, *not yours*. Getting all huffy and insulted and starting an argument when you try to reason with her is an abuser's way of diverting your attention from the *real* issue, so that she can avoid having to apologize or agree to any changes in her behavior. In fact, if she's really good at her little act, she'll wind up getting *you* to apologize for upsetting *her*! This will also guarantee that in the future, you'll be reluctant to ever again bring up anything else you might need to get resolved with her.

Your challenge, on the other hand, is to turn the tables on this strategy and make the confrontation so unpleasant for *her* that she'll be the one who is reluctant to rattle *your* cage again. If you succeed, there actually might be a chance that you'll be able to resume a reasonably pleasant relationship with this person. Because, if nothing else, at least she'll have gained some respect for you and will hopefully be more careful about ignoring your boundaries in the future. If you can get her to censor what she says and does around you in the future, then your interactions will at least be tolerable, should you choose to continue in the relationship or be stuck with it temporarily until you can make your escape. And whatever it takes to accomplish that might be worth a try. Again, although it is not the first and best choice, you can love your friend or relative and still rebuke her severely, if her own hard-hearted nature makes it necessary.

When rebuking a fellow believer, by all means, point out what the Bible says about her behavior. If she lacks this understanding, it would be helpful to lovingly explain how her sin will separate her from God. Unfortunately this very crucial point, which means so much to us as Christians, will have absolutely no effect on a non-believer. Those who have no relationship with the Lord to begin with aren't going to care about damaging something that doesn't exist. When the offender is a non-believer, the strongest motivations for her to change will be exposure, embarrassment, social censure, and the disapproval of her peers. You will find this is true of some "Christians" as well. But since we are Christians, no matter whom we are rebuking, it is important for us to make it clear that we do not condone abusive behavior, and that we strongly disapprove of wickedness.

The one you are rebuking may very well believe that you are not being loving, and may accuse you of "harshness", "attacking" her, etc. But just because she *feels* unloved at this particular time, does not mean it's true. You can tell her you are sorry she feels that way, but that doesn't change the fact that what *she* did was wrong and you do not accept it. Such a reaction is the result of her own pride and the shame she feels at being confronted with her own unacceptable behavior. Rather than learn from your rebuke and repent, she chooses to try and turn it around to make *you* feel guilty for speaking up to her. An abuser's negative reaction does not mean that we were wrong for rebuking her. Her reaction really doesn't matter. It is not our job to make her happy at the price of turning a blind eye to her wrongdoing. Our only obligation is to be obedient to the Lord, and to stand up and confront wickedness as he has told us to do.

Here are some examples of rebuke in some common situations. First, I have given the mild version (A), and secondly, the more forceful version of these examples (B), for when the milder versions won't work. These are just examples of dialog to demonstrate how rebuke might sound. The potential situations which might call for rebuke are endless and it is impossible to give exact examples to cover every circumstance, but I hope to give you some ideas as a jumping-off point:

(A) "It was wrong of you to keep that money when the clerk gave you too much change. What if it comes out of the clerk's pocket? You need to give it back."

(B) "It is dishonest of you not to return that money. That's stealing. I'm ashamed of you."

(A) "You embarrassed me when you told Aunt Snoopy about my marital problems. You broke a confidence, and now I feel as if I can't trust you anymore."

(B) "How dare you tell anyone my personal business? It's not your place to talk about me to others. If I want anyone to know my business, I'll tell them myself. Don't do it again."

(A) "I know you don't realize this, but when you've been drinking, your behavior is inappropriate and your judgment is poor. So you cannot be with my children if you've had a drink."

(B) "Being drunk in front of the children is totally unacceptable. You are never to drink in their presence again."

(A) "I don't like it when you raise your voice to me. Let's stop this conversation now and pick it up again after we've both calmed down."

(B) "I am another adult, not a naughty child you think you can yell at. From now on, you will address me with respect, or I will hang up (or leave). Is that clear?"

(A) "Maybe you didn't mean to hurt Claire's feelings, but what you said to her sounded a lot like criticism. I think you owe her an apology."

(B) "Sometimes you say very hurtful things and you need to keep that in check when talking to Claire. No one really wants to hear your criticisms. You need to apologize to her for what you said."

(A) "Let's try and make our get-togethers enjoyable for both of us. I don't want to spend our time together listening to you evaluate me, so please stop."

(B) "If you are going to be judgmental of my life, then you need to keep your opinions to yourself. What I do is none of your business."

(A) "How could you say that about Henry? You know it's not true. You need to go back and set the record straight."

(B) "You lied and passed malicious gossip around about Henry. I will not let you get away with hurting his reputation.

You need to go back and admit to everyone that you just made it up, or I will."

(A) "Mom, sometimes you have to take other people's wishes into consideration."
(B) "Mom, you are being selfish and demanding. It's not all about you."

Sometimes, there are situations in which the behavior is just so wrong that a mild rebuke would be inappropriate. These are times we need to be direct and tell the offender in plain language that he is *wrong*! Only forceful rebuke fits certain circumstances:

* "You used my apartment to cheat on your wife? I'm not going to let you involve me in your adultery. Give me my key back now- you're not welcome here anymore."
* "I know you hit Portia. Your behavior is deplorable. The next time I hear about anything like this, I will call the police on you, whether Portia wants me to or not."
* "No, I'm not your friend since you were convicted of child molestation. I don't have pedophiles for friends."
* "How can you still have anything to do with Slimeball now that he's in prison for raping your daughter? That's disgusting. As long as you continue to support the pervert who raped your own child, I will have nothing to do with you."
* "You stole money from your sister?! That is really despicable. If you don't return it immediately, I will tell her what you did."

Mild or forceful, rebuke of a truly wicked person has little chance of actually working. The Bible tells us not to bother rebuking fools who will not listen. After we rebuke them once or twice, their reaction will tell us whether they are "fools" or not. And if they are, we are not supposed to keep trying. We are supposed to avoid them from then on. The point of rebuke is to correct and help turn from sin those who will listen, and to at least stand up to the evil of those who will not. The Lord's judgment is righteous and perfect, and all who continue in their evil ways will be punished. Our job is to rebuke wrongdoers, for their own sakes, and to try to influence them to repent. But God does not tell us to try forever. Once we have given an offender fair warning that his behavior is wrong, if he remains stubborn and continues in his sin, then we are to give up and let him be. The Lord will deal with him after that.

PEOPLE WHO ACCEPT CORRECTION ARE ON THE PATHWAY TO LIFE, BUT THOSE WHO IGNORE IT WILL LEAD OTHERS ASTRAY...Proverbs 10:17 NLT.

HE WHO LISTENS TO A LIFE-GIVING REBUKE WILL BE AT HOME AMONG THE WISE. HE WHO IGNORES DISCIPLINE DESPISES HIMSELF, BUT WHOEVER HEEDS CORRECTION GAINS UNDERSTANDING.....Proverbs 15:31-32 NIV.

Chapter 12

When I Rebuked Their Evil, They Told Me I Was Not Supposed to Judge

Those we rebuke and their Flying Monkeys will usually try to divert attention off of *their* wrongdoing by accusing *us* of doing something wrong when we dare to speak up to them. When we confront them for their abuse, one common reaction is to accuse us of "judging" them. Turning it around and twisting scripture by telling us we're not supposed to "judge" is neither an appropriate response nor a defense for committing evil, when what is called for is an apology and repentance.

Actually, the Bible says that we, the saints of God, *are* supposed to judge. We are to judge both those in the world and those in the church:

DARE ANY OF YOU, HAVING A MATTER AGAINST ANOTHER, GO TO LAW BEFORE THE UNJUST, AND NOT BEFORE THE SAINTS? **DO YE NOT KNOW THAT THE SAINTS SHALL JUDGE THE WORLD?** *AND IF THE WORLD SHALL BE JUDGED BY YOU, ARE YE UNWORTHY TO JUDGE THE SMALLEST MATTERS? KNOW YE NOT THAT WE SHALL JUDGE ANGELS? HOW MUCH MORE*

THINGS THAT PERTAIN TO THIS LIFE? ...1Corinthians 6:1-3 KJV.

Furthermore, the spiritual man judges all things, but he himself is not subject to the judgment of any other man. The children of God have the mind of Christ, so yes, we are ordained to judge :

*NOW WE HAVE RECEIVED, NOT THE SPIRIT OF THE WORLD, BUT THE SPIRIT WHICH IS OF GOD; THAT WE MIGHT KNOW THE THINGS THAT ARE FREELY GIVEN TO US OF GOD. WHICH THINGS ALSO WE SPEAK, NOT IN THE WORDS WHICH MAN'S WISDOM TEACHETH, BUT WHICH THE HOLY GHOST TEACHETH; COMPARING SPIRITUAL THINGS WITH SPIRITUAL. BUT THE NATURAL MAN RECEIVETH NOT THE THINGS OF THE SPIRIT OF GOD: FOR THEY ARE FOOLISHNESS UNTO HIM: NEITHER CAN HE KNOW THEM, BECAUSE THEY ARE SPIRITUALLY DISCERNED. **BUT HE THAT IS SPIRITUAL JUDGETH ALL THINGS, YET HE HIMSELF IS JUDGED OF NO MAN.** FOR WHO HATH KNOWN THE MIND OF THE LORD, THAT HE MAY INSTRUCT HIM? **BUT WE HAVE THE MIND OF CHRIST**...1Corinthians 2:12-16 KJV.*

The Bible teaches us not to judge merely by appearances. This can be applied when deciding whether or not the person who offended us is a true "brother" or "sister" in Christ, or a phony one. Plenty of fake "Christians" are able to quote Scripture to appear "godly" and impress other people with their "righteousness," but they give themselves away by being unable to grasp the true spiritual meaning of those same scriptures. Note this verse does not say "do not judge," it says to judge righteously:

*JUDGE NOT ACCORDING TO THE APPEARANCE, BUT
JUDGE RIGHTEOUS JUDGMENT...John 7:24 KJV.*

Rebuking is in fact righteous, godly judging, which we are instructed to do. What is ungodly judging? It might help to make this distinction between godly and ungodly judging: godly judgment and godly rebuke are based on *facts*, while ungodly judgment is based on *assumptions*. In other words, when you disapprove of/ protest/ confront an abuser for behaving in ways that hurt other people (fact), and he responds by accusing you of not being a good Christian (assumption), because you are confronting him, "judging" him, "not honoring" him, not being "loving," etc., etc., *then you are* **rebuking** *him, but he is* **"judging"** *you*. More specifically, you are rendering righteous and godly judgment on him; however, he is doing exactly what he is falsely accusing you of doing~ judging you *unrighteously and without godly authority.*

Chapter 13

Repentance and Apologies

FOOLS MOCK AT MAKING AMENDS FOR SIN, BUT GOODWILL IS FOUND AMONG THE UPRIGHT....Proverbs 14:9 NIV.

REPENT: To change from past evil; to feel such regret for what one has done as to dedicate oneself to changing one's life; to abandon one's evil ways; to change for the better as a result of remorse for past behavior.

*"AND JESUS SAID UNTO HER, NEITHER DO I CONDEMN THEE: **GO, AND SIN NO MORE**"...John 8:11 KJV.*

When Jesus forgave the adulteress in John Chapter 8, he said, "Go, *and sin no more.*" He did *not* say, "I forgive you this time, now go right back to what you were doing wrong, and every time you do more evil, just come on back and I'll forgive you again." In order for her to merit forgiveness, Jesus required *change* (repentance).

A sincere apology and the changing of one's hurtful ways, along with a little time, is often all it takes to restore trust in a damaged or lost relationship. Normal folks have no problem smoothing things over, making amends for an offense, and being remorseful for hurting someone who loves them, especially if it means being able to stay on good terms and keep the relationship intact. It seems so simple. And it's the only possible way to restore the damaged bond. So, why the abuser's extreme reluctance to do it?

Abusers, narcissists and control freaks love having the upper hand. Humbling themselves to sincerely apologize is rarely something they're willing to do, much less commit to a change in behavior. For one thing, making amends would mean swallowing their pride, which would just about kill them. It would also require effort on their parts. And the sad truth is that, to them, we're just not worth that effort.

You see, they know something we don't know. They know that our bond with them is not based on love. It's based on domination, codependency, fear, resistance to change, and addiction, with a little Stockholm Syndrome thrown in for good measure. They know from past experience that *they don't have to treat us well.* They can treat us like garbage, and we'll still stick around for more. They have no motivation at all to apologize or change their ways, because they don't take us seriously. And they don't care one bit about our feelings.

But with God's grace, we can find the courage to change our lives for the better, with or without our abuser's cooperation. An important step in deciding whether to stay in a relationship, or end it, is learning to recognize sincere apologies and true remorse, and understanding that these are essential to replacing our one-way, toxic relationship with a healthy bond.

LET THE WICKED FORSAKE HIS WAY AND THE UNRIGHTEOUS MAN HIS THOUGHTS; AND LET HIM RETURN TO THE LORD, AND HE WILL HAVE COMPASSION ON HIM,

AND TO OUR GOD, FOR HE WILL ABUNDANTLY PARDON....
Isaiah 55:7 NASB.

BUT BECAUSE OF YOUR STUBBORNNESS AND YOUR UNREPENTANT HEART, YOU ARE STORING UP WRATH AGAINST YOURSELF FOR THE DAY OF GOD'S WRATH, WHEN HIS RIGHTEOUS JUDGMENT WILL BE REVEALED. GOD WILL GIVE TO EACH PERSON ACCORDING TO WHAT HE HAS DONE.....Romans 2:5-6 NIV.

Chapter 14

Meaningful vs. Meaningless Apologies

Meaningless apologies are given for the purpose of benefiting the offender in some way, instead of helping the victim to feel better.** They only pay lip service to being sorry, but there is no actual remorse. They are an attempt to just "get it over with," while allowing the abuser to come out of it looking good, with his pride and dignity still intact. They are often intended to subtly make the victim look unreasonable and in the wrong- to make her seem like the *real* guilty party, who will not be "satisfied" with an apology and is still "carrying a grudge."

Unfortunately, much of what defines an abuser is extreme selfishness and an exaggerated sense of entitlement, rather than humility and a genuine concern for others. *Much to the surprise of many abusers, they are **not** entitled to forgiveness merely on the basis of an empty, trite, worthless, or insincere apology.*

As we have already discussed, God requires us to forgive whenever there is repentance, just as he forgives us when we come to him and repent. However, *a mere apology does **not** constitute repentance.* Repentance takes more effort than that. Repentance means *change.* It also means trying to right the wrong you did- making restitution, restoring the reputation of one you lied about, etc., When one who has victimized us has demonstrated that he *truly regrets* what he has done, and that he has *turned from his abusive behavior and dedicated himself to changing his ways*- only then are we scripturally required to forgive. And although we are required to forgive if he properly repents, keep in mind that *we are still not required to reconcile.*

A meaningful apology is primarily concerned with righting the wrong that was done. Someone who gives a meaningful apology makes it crystal clear that *the feelings of the victim are her top priority.* By apologizing, she is not trying to make herself look good, or to benefit herself in any way. She is humble, truly remorseful, and willing to do whatever is needed to make amends. She understands and accepts that her apology may not restore the relationship, but she is not doing it to accomplish her own purposes or to fulfill her own needs, wishes, or desires. *She is doing it to help the victim heal*- emotionally, mentally, and spiritually- from the damage and pain she inflicted with her abuse, betrayal, or offensive behavior or words. Unless we have received a genuine apology and evidence of repentance (which may take time to observe), there is no obligation to forgive.

IF YOU HAVE BEEN SNARED WITH THE WORDS OF YOUR MOUTH, HAVE BEEN CAUGHT WITH THE WORDS OF YOUR MOUTH, DO THIS THEN, MY SON, AND DELIVER YOURSELF; SINCE YOU HAVE COME INTO THE HAND OF YOUR NEIGHBOR. GO, HUMBLE YOURSELF, AND IMPORTUNE YOUR NEIGHBOR. GIVE NO SLEEP TO YOUR EYES, NOR SLUMBER TO YOUR EYELIDS; DELIVER YOURSELF, LIKE A GAZELLE FROM THE HUNTER'S HAND AND LIKE A BIRD FROM THE HAND OF THE FOWLER... Proverbs 6:2-5 NASB.

AND THE LORD SPOKE TO MOSES, SAYING, "SPEAK TO THE CHILDREN OF ISRAEL: 'WHEN A MAN OR WOMAN COMMITS ANY SIN THAT MEN COMMIT IN

UNFAITHFULNESS AGAINST THE LORD, AND THAT PERSON IS GUILTY, THEN HE SHALL CONFESS THE SIN WHICH HE HAS COMMITTED. HE SHALL MAKE RESTITUTION FOR HIS TRESPASS IN FULL, PLUS ONE-FIFTH OF IT, AND GIVE IT TO THE ONE HE HAS WRONGED".....Numbers 5:5-7 NKJV.

IF A FIRE BREAK OUT, AND CATCH IN THORNS, SO THAT THE STACKS OF CORN, OR THE STANDING CORN, OR THE FIELD, BE CONSUMED THEREWITH; HE THAT KINDLED THE FIRE SHALL SURELY MAKE RESTITUTION....Exodus 22:6 KJV.

HE THAT COVERETH HIS SINS SHALL NOT PROSPER: BUT WHOSO CONFESSETH AND FORESAKETH THEM SHALL HAVE MERCY...Proverbs 28:13 KJV.

Chapter 15

"But I've Changed, so You Have to Give Me Another Chance"

Sisters and Brothers, do any of these lines ring a bell with you?:

*   "I've changed."
*   "I'm a new person."
*   "I don't do those things anymore."
*   "I don't act like that anymore."
*   "The Lord has worked a change in my heart."
*   "I've turned over a new leaf."
*   "I'm not like I was before."
*   "I'm a different person than I once was."
*   "That was in the past."
*   "I promise I'm a changed man/woman."
*   "I've learned my lesson."
*   "That was the old me, this is the new me."
*   "Things are different now."

Most of us have heard the above assurances at some time in our lives, usually in one of two situations:

1. Either we've gotten fed up with our abuser and he knows we are getting ready to end the relationship,
    Or,
2. The relationship already ended some time previously, we haven't spoken to our abuser in a while and thought she was out of our lives. But meanwhile, she's getting impatient waiting for us to "come around," so she decided to try again.

When we fail to jump at the chance to have our abuser back in our lives, he will usually turn up the pressure with such statements as:

*   "You *have to* believe me/ give me one more chance/ another shot/ the benefit of the doubt/ trust me/ let me prove it to you, etc."
*   "You *have to* forgive and forget."
*   "Let's move on."
*   "Let's start fresh."
*   "Everybody deserves another chance."
*   "Just let bygones be bygones."
*   "It's time to get over it."

Then, should we continue to hesitate, or ask for more details on exactly what changes he's made, he will change tactics and cop an attitude, turning the tables and becoming impatient and angry with us, as if *we* have some nerve for hurting or insulting him:

*   "Why do you keep bringing up the past?"
*   "You *have to* stop harping on it."
*   "Why don't you believe me?"
*   "I can see I'm never going to hear the end of this."
*   "I worked very hard to get to this point and now you won't trust me."

* "Why are you so unreasonable?"
* "There's just no pleasing you."
* "You're *never* gonna let me forget it, are you?"
* "You'll never be satisfied until you see me beg."
* "What do you want from me?"
* "Look, I *told* you I changed! If you think I'm gonna kiss your butt, you can go to hell!"
* "Fine, *be* that way! If you're not gonna believe me, then just forget it! Some Christian *you* are!"

All of which proves he really didn't change at all, and we were right not to believe him or trust him.

In my book Narcissistic Confrontations, I told part of the story of the breakup of my relationship with a childhood friend who had become abusive, demanding, and controlling. The relationship ended over the course of a year and a half, during which a number of long e-mails were exchanged, containing several interesting recurring themes, which have been excellent examples of abusive reactions that we can all study and learn from.

One such recurring theme was this narcissist's repetitive, but meaningless and ultimately untrue, declarations of change. Many times, when I held her accountable for her selfishness or nastiness, she would respond that she "no longer acted that way," the implication being that I was "blaming" her for the way she used to act in the past.

In the course of trying to convince me to give her yet another chance, after many, many chances, she told me no less than eight times that she "no longer does those things", "no longer reacts the way she used to", "has repented to God for what she was doing wrong", "finally pulled down those things that were strongholds for her in the past", and "God has shown her where she needed to make changes and she has made those changes."

However, here's the interesting part. Because her statements were vague and never specified exactly what changes she had made or what behavior she no longer did, I felt I needed some more details in order to discern whether or not she was being truthful. So each time she claimed she had changed, I asked her to tell me what the Lord had shown her, what she was now doing differently, and *how* she had changed. Whereupon she would again become just as rude, nasty and hostile as before, *and exhibit every one of the offensive behaviors which I had originally set limits on and which she claimed to no longer be doing.*

It actually only took very little prodding for her façade to drop and her true colors to come out once again. The simple act of asking for clarification exposed her lies, prevented me from wasting any more time giving her fifth and sixth and twelfth and twentieth chances, and protected me from getting involved again with a jealous, demanding, high-maintenance, selfish narcissist.

Abusers think we should take their preposterous and often repetitive claims of repentance at face value. They don't get that trust cannot be turned on and off like a light switch, and that once they have damaged or destroyed our trust, they are going to have to put some time and effort into rebuilding it. They think if they simply repeat themselves enough times or raise their voices loud enough, it will make whatever hogwash they're trying to get us to buy more believable.

Control-freaks balk at the idea that they have to *earn* our trust. It rankles them that we are not going to reconcile with them until they have *proven* themselves, because this means that *we* are now in control, we are now making the rules, and we have taken the control away from them.

Narcissists think they are so wonderful that everyone should be grateful to be in their company. They believe they are entitled to anything they want. It is a foreign concept to them that they are *not* entitled to have a relationship with us unless they *deserve* it, and unless *we* want it, too.

DEAR FRIENDS, DO NOT BELIEVE EVERY SPIRIT, BUT TEST THE SPIRITS TO SEE WHETHER THEY ARE FROM GOD...1 John 4:1 NIV.

The Bible clearly tells us *not to believe* everyone, but to *test* people to see if they are operating in a godly spirit or a demonic spirit. Abusers become highly offended at the notion that we are testing them, and that we might not consider them a good risk or worthy of a relationship with us. But when they repeatedly fall back into their default mode of the same lame old empty promises and assurances, with never any actual concrete changes made, only to relapse time and again into their usual abusive behavior as soon as things don't go their way, we would have to be fools to believe their baloney without requiring proof of change. Like the old saying goes- fool me once, shame on you; fool me twice, shame on me!

So when your abuser lavishes you with vows of repentance, no matter how convincing she may sound, stop and remind yourself that talk is cheap, and that actions speak louder than words. Take your time and feel free to question her. Ask her to be specific about exactly how she has changed, what she realizes she was doing wrong, what behaviors she has stopped, and what hurtful things she no longer does to other people.

When I asked my ex-friend for examples of how she had changed, one tactic she used was to ask *me* to give *her* examples of her own behaviors so she could answer me. This is another nonsensical, crazy-making response so typical of abusers. First of all, how would I know what behavioral changes she had made? How could *I* tell *her* what the Lord had supposedly told her she needed to repent of? How on earth could I answer that question for her?

This response alone indicated that she was lying about really changing. She was just fishing for what I wanted to hear, so she could respond only to whatever she thought was important to me in deciding whether or not to reconcile with her. It brought to mind the way kids manipulate each other~ "You go first", "No, *you* go first." At the risk of sounding like one of those kids, "I asked her first!" I didn't want to give her the ability to merely pretend that whatever was important to me just happened to be the things she changed. I wanted to hear the *truth*. And that would not have happened had I let her maneuver me into answering my own question for her.

Obviously, if I gave her the examples of unacceptable behaviors which I had asked her to give to *me*, that would get her off the hook from actually having to do any introspection. Abusers are experts at taking the easy way out of being held responsible for their own behavior. She would have just pretended to agree with whatever I was saying, or she would have twisted what I was saying into another excuse to avoid accountability. But she would not have been required to back up her statement of change with anything of substance that would prove she really *had* changed.

So I simply told her I couldn't accommodate her and would have no way of knowing the answers to what she had learned from her own introspection. This caused her to drop her pretense of change and have another narcissistic meltdown. After several episodes of going around in circles like this, I was able to reach the decision to permanently cut off contact, knowing that I was only rewarding her narcissism by continuing to give her the attention she was manipulating me into giving her. At that point I realized she was a liar and I wasn't going to play her games anymore.

So when deciding whether or not to reconcile with an abuser, take your time and don't allow yourself to be pressured into making a hasty and premature decision. Don't settle for empty promises, vague assurances and evasive answers. Insist on details. Ask him to describe exactly how he has changed. Then listen and observe. Is he willing to put forth the effort needed to earn your trust? Is he being truthful? Does he agree that you have every right to question him, and that he can't blame you for not believing him right away? Does he respectfully answer your questions while remaining calm, sincere and remorseful? Or does he become angry, defensive, "insulted" or outraged? His responses will tell you whether he is genuinely remorseful and repentant, or just manipulating you, lying to you, and telling you whatever he thinks you want to hear so he can weasel his way back into your life. Do not allow yourself to be steamrolled back into a relationship that is not beneficial for *you*.

Here are some helpful guidelines for discerning whether your abuser has *really* turned over a new leaf, or if he's just trying to con you into taking him back without any real effort or commitment on his part to change his ways:

1. Don't be a fool and don't make it easy. Be skeptical and ask for details. When an abuser claims he's changed, don't just accept his statement with no further explanation. Say, "Really? *How* have you changed?", "What exactly do you mean by that?", "That's nice. What specific changes have you made?" or even, "I'm listening........" Then be quiet and let him explain. Let him put some effort into proving he's repented.

2. Ask open-ended questions and be careful not to answer them for the abuser. Some abusers are very clever at fishing for what we really want to hear and tricking us into giving them the answers which they then spoon-feed back to us. For example, in response to her statement that "I've changed," don't *you* say, "So you're going to stop criticizing me?", "So now you understand that I can't call you back right away all the time?", or, "Well I'm glad you realize that lying upsets me and you're not going to do it anymore." If you do this, you just gave your abuser the opportunity to respond with a simple "yes" that will satisfy you while requiring no actual introspection or thought

from her. This is not a serious commitment to change on her part. In other words, when your abuser claims she's changed, don't *you* tell *her* how she's changed. Make *her* tell *you*. Make her justify and explain her statement of change so you can better determine how serious she is and how truthful she's being.

3. After you've heard what she has to say for herself, don't be afraid to ask more questions. Force your abuser to be very specific about the changes she's made in her life and her behavior towards you and others. If the only thing you get from her is evasive or vague answers, then say, "I really don't think you've given this enough thought. Get back to me when you have something more specific to tell me, and we'll discuss it then."

4. Make your "chat" short and sweet. Get right down to business, and don't get sidetracked. Don't allow your abuser to stay connected to you by keeping you talking and discussing when you have not yet decided whether or not to renew the relationship. If you let him involve you in a long talk at this point, you are *rewarding* him by talking to him before he *deserves* to be rewarded. Maintain the upper hand. If he cannot tell you precisely and in detail how he's changed himself, then end the conversation until such time as he can come back to you with the kinds of answers you're looking for.

5. If he has given real thought to making changes, and is able to give you details, don't hesitate to buy yourself time anyway. You don't have to forgive him on the spot, or take him back. You're allowed to have time to think it over. Tell him you appreciate his efforts at repentance, you need to think it over, and that you'll get back to him after you've made a decision.

6. Both during and after your discussion, keep your antennae up, observe closely, and consider carefully the abuser's

words, unspoken messages, attitude, facial expressions and body language. Did you see signs of genuine godly remorse? Or was she resentful that she was being forced to answer to you? Did she become impatient? Was there feeling behind her words, or was she cool, aloof, or detached? If she displayed feeling or emotion, did you get the impression it was sincere, or phony? Were her claims of repentance given grudgingly, or was she cooperative, genuinely loving, and eager to prove herself to you?

7. Make him work for it. Don't be a push-over. It's okay to make him squirm. If you make it too easy, he'll soon forget all his promises and go back to mistreating you. He'll learn that the next time he pushes you too far, all he has to do to con you is to *pretend* he's seen the error of his ways and make a few empty promises, and you'll take him back again. He'll know that he can keep repeating this cycle over and over again, forever, and always trick you into giving him another chance. This removes all incentive for *real*, genuine change. If he has to work for it, he'll appreciate your forgiveness more, and think twice before risking your goodwill and getting on your bad side again.

8. This little "dance," if done successfully, will result in a role-reversal of control and power in the relationship. Knowing that you are hesitant to give him another chance, and, indeed, might *not* give him another chance, upsets a narcissist's equilibrium. He thought you adored him so much that you'd put up with anything, but now he's not so sure. It's good to make him think that you're not all that eager to take him back. The next time he upsets you might be the last time, because obviously you're not as crazy about him as he thought. Seeing that you're willing to walk away from the relationship if he doesn't keep you happy puts a whole new spin on things. It shifts the power to you. He should be grateful to you for giving him one last chance. If he has

really changed, then he'll have nothing to worry about. But if he's lying, he'll be more likely to at least make an effort to walk on eggshells, knowing that the next time he offends you, he just might get kicked to the curb permanently.

Many of us go through months and years of uncertainty before finally going strict No Contact with narcissistic relatives and friends. Unfortunately we have feelings for the narcissists and abusers in our lives, and it can take quite a while for us to be ready to stop wasting our lives and permanently let them go. When abusive family members or friends pop up again after a period of estrangement, it is not because they love us and miss us. *It's because they want something from us. In fact, it is often triggered by them losing one of their other sources of narcissistic supply* (another relationship they were feeding off of broke up), so they start looking up their old, already-housebroken victims and trying to resurrect them as targets again.

When a narcissist contacts us again after an estrangement, she will be on her best behavior and we might be tempted to believe her claims of change. But remember, first and foremost, *all narcissists are liars.* I have never known a narcissist to be able to keep up the "nice" act and the pretense of change for more than six months to a year without slipping up and letting you catch at least one telltale fleeting glimpse (yes, it will be quick, so keep your eyes open or you might miss it) of her true colors once again. That is, if she doesn't just give up all pretense once she has you back and completely revert to type. Time is your friend here, so delay for a very long time before letting an estranged friend or relative back into your life. Be patient, watch and wait. Buy all the time you need to be sure that any changes the narcissist claims to have made are real and permanent. By the time you realize you are still being played, maybe you will be ready to take that next big step, go strict No Contact, and move on forever to a narcissist-free life.

Chapter 16

Can One Person Apologize for Somebody Else?

WHOSO DIGGETH A PIT SHALL FALL THEREIN: AND HE THAT ROLLETH A STONE, IT WILL RETURN UPON HIM.... Proverbs 26:27 KJV.

IF A MAN PAYS BACK EVIL FOR GOOD, EVIL WILL NEVER LEAVE HIS HOUSE....Proverbs 17:13 NIV.

It never ceases to amaze me how many ripples and ramifications our abuser's behavior can have for all concerned. And how, against our wishes and through no fault of our own, we can be forced into all kinds of uncomfortable predicaments, both in the present and for years to come. The typical abuser's selfish and cunning habit of lying about us and smearing us to the rest of the family, combined with her Flying Monkeys' self-righteous tendency to judge us and take sides against us rather than remaining neutral, butting out, or, God forbid, defending us, often lead to future complications that no one ever anticipated.

In their rush to disapprove of and punish us for setting limits and refusing to tolerate any more of their abuse, our abusers and their Monkeys often fail to consider how their actions might backfire on *them* later on. Here we will discuss one of the most classic dilemmas that the family abusers' and budinskis' typical lack of foresight can lead to down to the road. It is more common in family situations than in other toxic groups; in fact, it's almost universal in family estrangements. Sooner or later almost every Adult Child or escapee will find herself in this situation.

Question: My mother was always abusive, jealous, and controlling. When I met my husband, she took an instant dislike to him, was openly hostile, insulted him to his face many times, and did every-thing she could to break us up. She was adamantly opposed to our wedding and threatened to disrupt it in any way she could- includ-ing standing up and objecting when the minister asked if anyone knew of any reason why we should not marry. Because of her behavior and threats, we decided not to invite her to our wedding. We could not take a chance on our wedding day being ruined and everyone being embarrassed by the things she said she would do.

When we refused to allow her to come to our wedding, she tried to turn the rest of my family against us. My aunt (her sis-ter), uncle, and their children all took her side and boycotted our wedding, and they have not spoken to us since.

It is now almost five years later, and my husband and I have a child and another one on the way. My mother seems to have had a change of heart with the birth of her grandchild. A few months ago, she called and asked to meet with my husband and me. She apologized to both of us for her behavior and took full responsibil-ity. She even said she doesn't blame us for not letting her attend our wedding after the threats she made to ruin it. She seems to have made some real changes in her attitude and is trying to mend fences. We are taking it slow and are hopeful that maybe we can trust her at some point and have a good relationship in the future.

Now here is the problem. It seems that my aunt and uncle and their children think that just because we have reconciled with my mother, it automatically means that *they* are included in the reconciliation, even though they have not apologized or done anything at all to make amends. I think my mother agrees with them but is not really saying anything because she knows our connection is shaky right now and she doesn't want to rock the boat.

For the last four years my mother has spent the holidays with them, but now she wants to spend them with us. And she wants my aunt and uncle to be included because one of their children moved out of state and the other one will be traveling, so this year they will be alone. This idea makes me and my husband extremely uncomfortable. We do not want to spend our holidays with people who betrayed us, took sides against us, spread gossip and lies about us, boycotted our wedding, and haven't spoken to us in five years. We don't trust my aunt and uncle, we feel they disapprove of us and don't even care that they hurt us, and we have no desire at all to be in their company.

When we agreed to accept my mother's apology and give her another chance, we did not know that she was part of a package deal with her sister and her family. I realize that it's not my fault that my mother dragged her sister and her family into our disagreement, and it's not my fault that my aunt took my mother's side and "punished" me. But I feel like *I'm* expected to pay the price for *their* decisions and overlook my aunt and her family's behavior, without them ever personally apologizing or admitting they did anything wrong. Does my mother's apology cover *them?* Does making up with my mother mean that her "supporters" are automatically included in our reconciliation? I'm getting the feeling that my mother's expectations in this situation are very different from mine.

Answer: An apology is not just an expression of remorse. *It is also an acceptance of responsibility.* How would it be possible for someone to accept responsibility for what somebody else did?

Wouldn't it be a little irrational on our part to *blame* one person for another's behavior? Of course it would. Then it follows that it would also be irrational to *forgive* someone who did wrong based on the apology of a third party. The only person who could justifiably apologize for another person would be the parent of a naughty child, who actually *is* responsible for her child's behavior.

I am a big proponent of personal responsibility, and of standing up and being accountable for one's own words and actions. I also greatly believe in letting Natural Consequences take their course and teach offenders a lesson that would be lost on them if we stepped in and bailed them out or let them off the hook too easily.

The problem that we face as Adult Children of narcissists or psychopaths is having been raised to continually overlook abuse, stuff our hurt down, not complain, and allow life to go on without upsetting the apple cart. In other words, to let our abusers get away with anything and everything, never apologize and never take any responsibility. We are expected to never "hurt the feelings" of those who deliberately trample all over ours. We have been indoctrinated into not rocking the boat and keeping the "peace" at all costs, even to our own detriment. Furthermore, we have been brainwashed into thinking that *the entire responsibility* for said "peace" is ours and ours alone, while nobody else does a thing to contribute to peaceful family relationships. Instead, it is perfectly acceptable if *everybody else except us* abuses, instigates, enables, and does everything possible to cause trouble at every turn.

The concepts of "justice" and "accountability" were unheard of in our families. *We* were always expected to forgive, regardless of the fact that no one even asked for forgiveness- because asking for forgiveness would mean swallowing pride and admitting fault. We have always been the family scapegoats; the onus was always on *us* to make it right and to take responsibility for *someone else's* behavior and the results of it. *The sole responsibility for keeping the peace at any cost has always been on our shoulders and our shoulders alone.* Ingraining this fallacy into our brains was very advantageous for our abusers, and worked very well for them for many years. Until now.

Now it's time to *unlearn* the false teachings of our childhoods. Now it's time to undo the indoctrination and the brainwashing that always seems to benefit our abusers at our expense. The truth is, *it is **not** our duty to "keep the peace" and constantly overlook evil behavior while our abusers have a field day victimizing us and stabbing us in the back.* If we forgive people who never even bother to *ask* for forgiveness, then we are undermining God's Law of Sowing and Reaping. We are giving them carte blanche to cause as much pain and suffering as they like, without ever having to answer for it.

What this means to the person who asked this question is that yes, it is not your fault that your mother dragged your aunt and uncle into your disagreement. *That's between your mother and your aunt and uncle,* although your mother's apology to you does also need to include an apology for any lies she told and for gossiping about you and turning other people against you. If your self-righteous aunt now finds herself in an awkward position concerning you, then she needs to take it up with *her sister,* the person who put her in that position. She also needs to accept responsibility for *her own* decision- which was to get involved and take sides when she should have butted out.

Your aunt and uncle need to apologize to you for shunning you and boycotting your wedding, and if they are embarrassed or angry at having to do this, *then your mother can apologize to them* for dragging them into this whole mess. These are two separate issues. One has nothing to do with the other. The first issue involves *you,* and is between *you* and your aunt and uncle. The second issue *does not involve you.* It is between *your mother* and your aunt and uncle.

Your aunt (and uncle) betrayed you, and they both owe you an apology for that. Their actions are not automatically covered by your mother's apology. Just because you reconcile with one estranged relative or friend does not mean the rest of the clan is automatically included, without ever having to be accountable and express remorse for their own actions. You wouldn't hold your *mother* responsible if your aunt or uncle wronged you. So how can your mother make amends for their behavior?

It is natural for us to feel uncomfortable around people we can't trust. This is an inborn, self-protective instinct that God gave us. How can we possibly feel comfortable again in the presence of people who we loved all our lives, but who cared so little for us that they would cut us out of *their* lives without batting an eye, just to please someone else? How can we possibly ever trust someone who would stab us in the back just to gain the approval of another person? Someone who, instead of defending us, giving us the benefit of the doubt, or at least remaining neutral, is perfectly okay with causing us pain and sorrow and never seeing us again, even though we never did anything at all to her- all just to stay on the good side of an abuser?

Why would we open ourselves again to a Judas who would sell us out at the drop of a hat? Why should we have to feel hypocritical and unsafe, forcing ourselves to smile and be nice, trying to make small talk with a backstabber who is so eager to judge us and believe lies and gossip about us? This is not our burden. We didn't *cause* this situation, and we need not allow ourselves to be burdened with *fixing* it. At some point, don't we have to start having some standards for the kinds of people we'll agree to have a relationship with? Like maybe that they need to have some loyalty? And integrity?

The Herd Mentality Of Abusive Groups

Sometimes I have to shake my head and ask myself, "How old are these people, anyway?" Twelve? I'm picturing a nasty little clique of whiny, immature schoolgirls- "*I'm* mad at Sally, so if you wanna be my friend, then *you* have to be mad at her too!" Or, "*I* don't talk to Jane, so *you* can't either!" Or, "Eeew, don't go near Beth! She's got cooties!" Silly, isn't it? When the parties involved are eight years old. When they're in their thirties, forties, fifties and beyond, it's petty, spiteful, ridiculous, bizarre and downright creepy.

What is going on with grown-ups who behave like mean, childish little brats? Who ever heard of a functional adult who, instead of fighting her own battles and resolving her own conflicts, has to "tattletale" like a little crybaby on the person she's "mad at," spreading gossip and lies and making it some kind of loyalty test to drag others into her problems and see whose side they'll choose?

Who ever heard of a normal adult who allows a third party to influence or force her to break up her relationship with someone else? Who stops talking to a friend or family member based on the say-so of someone who is obviously angry and upset with said friend or family member, and therefore more likely to lie or exaggerate to make the first one seem like a terrible person and whatever happened between them sound much worse than it really was? Who would be foolish enough to take such accusations at face value, and actually *end* her relationship with someone because of what is supposedly going on between him and somebody else?

Well, normal, functional adults wouldn't do these things- and don't do them. But we're not talking normal here. We're talking narcissistic, abusive, psychotic nut-jobs. And their world is a whole different world from the rest of ours.

What are they thinking? They're *not* thinking, at least not rationally. If they were, they'd be coming up with constructive suggestions for the bully to change her behavior, instead of agreeing with her, egging her on, and adding fuel to the fire.

Just as a single narcissistic abuser refuses to allow others their autonomy apart from him, the abusive narcissistic family or group does not see and accept each member as a separate individual. The uniqueness of each person and the differences between them are not celebrated. Instead, individuality and free thinking are perceived as threatening, and not allowed. Everyone is just part of one larger sick organism- kind of like a big, ugly, smoldering, rotten lump. This thing moves as one, thinks as one, acts as one. One part cannot separate itself from the lump and speak out on its own. All the parts have to agree with what the other parts say. Because they are not emotionally separate individuals, but merely enmeshed parts of one big whole.

Nobody in such a family or group thinks for themselves. There is one way of thinking, one collective decision-making process, one opinion for all of them. Anyone who breaks from the group mentality will become an outsider, quick to be shut up or shunned. If you want to be an insider and remain in the good graces of the big ugly lump of enmeshed parts, then you can have no mind of your own. You have no choice but to go along with the group and be of one mind with them. Being right or wrong doesn't matter. The only thing that matters is *being the same.*

The abusive family's idea of togetherness is a totalitarian vision carried to the extreme. It's one for all and all for one, a kind of weird Cold War regime where a select few people dictate what everyone else has to think, say, and do. And the Flying Monkey "secret police" keep an eye on everybody and keep them all in line, reporting any signs of independent thinking and carrying out the necessary "dissuasion."

In their warped pathological perception, if you offend *one* of them, you offended them *all.* If you set a boundary or stand up and say something to one, it's as if you said it to the whole tribe. If one is mad at you, they're all mad at you. If one isn't speaking to you, they're all not speaking to you. And if one suddenly ups and decides that they *are* speaking to you again, then *everybody* is speaking to you again. The only wild card they never consider is whether *you* will want to speak to *them* again. They simply assume that you will passively go along with whatever the group decides. Just like all of them do.

Think of lemmings, all following each other to their deaths off the cliff, never stopping for a second and saying, "Hey, wait a minute. Maybe this isn't such a good idea after all! Maybe there's a better way." The same herd mentality auto-pilots our abusive families and other toxic groups. No one ever says "Hmmm...now, let's see. How will my taking sides and shunning so-and-so help resolve this situation?" No one has the brains or the foresight to think, "Hey, wait a minute! If I go along with betraying someone who never did anything bad to me, then what? How might this come back and bite me in the future? If I change my mind later on and want to make up, how will I undo what I did? If, some-where down the road, both of my feuding friends or relatives mend fences, where will that leave *me*?"

Thinking, speaking and acting as one big dysfunctional lump of lemmings, and blindly following whoever puts on the most the-atrical performance, our narcissistic relatives, church members, or friends manage to make sure that a disagreement between just two people, which might eventually have been resolved had it stayed limited, turns into a huge feud involving the whole fam-ily, the whole church, or the whole social circle, and causing hard feelings for years to come.

The chances of the original problem ever being resolved ami-cably drops exponentially with each additional person added to the mix. This results in rifts that can never be healed, and a group or family that will never be the same (which is probably a good thing!). Hence, this mother and aunt and uncle, for their own self-ish motivations, instigated trouble and caused a rift between their children that not only they, but all the cousins, will now have to live with.

They Know They're Wrong, So They Hide From You

If it's any consolation, one thing I've learned from this experience is not to take it personally when narcissists, abusers and psychopaths, especially the peripheral ones, disown you. Usually, the reason they disown you is not that *you* did something wrong, but that *they* did something wrong, like gossiping about you. And now they're either embarrassed at getting caught, too cowardly to deal with it when they *do* get caught, too ashamed to face you, afraid of your anger, or trying to discredit you by making *you* look bad before you can expose *them*. They don't want to have to answer for what they did, so they turn it all around and pretend that *you* hurt *them*. Then, like the morally deficient cowards they are, they make themselves scarce and get out of range before you can hold them accountable- and usually before you can even realize the full extent of what they did to you. When they disown you after doing something wrong to *you*, what they are really doing is hiding from you. They are not giving you the chance to rebuke them. If they keep refusing to speak to you, then how can you ever confront them or ask for an apology?

And of course, if they are shunning you, you will never have the opportunity to see any repentance (there isn't any in this situation to see). But the good thing is that hiding from you is another example of their own behavior backfiring on them, because without any evidence of repentance, you will therefore be scripturally precluded from forgiving them, and relieved of any obligation to do so.

How A Flying Monkey's Choices Can Wind Up Guaranteeing That There Will Never Be Peace In The Family Again

Now this is where things start getting sticky. Let's say that sometime in the future a narcissist regrets what she did, apologizes to her victim, and wants to make amends. Did she also snub the victim's children? Then she owes them an apology as well. She can't expect the victim to betray her own children and make up with someone who hurt them and never made it right. Did she bad-mouth the victim and cause her to be snubbed by other people? Then she needs to apologize for this, go to those other people and set the record straight, undo the damage she did, confess to any lies she made up, and restore those relationships that she ruined.

The only way a complete restoration could occur would be for everyone concerned to act like mature, accountable adults, take responsibility for what they did, and make amends for their own actions. No one else can do it for them. In order for everyone concerned to be able to attend family events together and be at peace in each other's company, then everyone concerned has to own up to what they've done and settle their own accounts.

That's sure a lot of apologizing that has to happen for such a rift to be healed and these relationships to be restored. Unfortunately, as all of us from abusive families, churches and social groups well know, the chances of any of this happening are nil. But if they fail to do this, just imagine attending the same get-together and socializing nicely with the relative who made amends, while still not being able to speak to those she turned against us, because *they* are still not speaking to *us!* A little ridiculous, isn't it?

To be forgiven, each individual needs to repent for what they have done. There is no such thing as "group forgiveness." There is no such thing as making up by default, sliding in on someone else's apology. *You cannot apologize by proxy. You cannot make amends by proxy. And you cannot forgive by proxy.* No one can speak for another person. No one can apologize for someone else, and no one can forgive for someone else.

So What Do I Do Now?

Going back to the person who asked the original question, it is normal and natural for you to feel uncomfortable spending a holiday with your aunt and uncle. However, you didn't create this awkward situation, and it's not up to you to fix it. You *can't* fix it, because you didn't cause it.

That leaves several options for your mother and aunt, the ones who *did* create the problem:

1. Your mother can choose to spend the holidays with her sister, and you and your family can have a nice peaceful, stress-free time without them.
2. Your mother can spend the holidays with you, if she wants to badly enough, and see her sister at another time.
3. Your aunt and uncle can apologize and show some sincere remorse to you and your husband, so that maybe you would be able to relax and feel at peace in their company. Then maybe you could all try celebrating Christmas together- if not just yet, then perhaps next year. If your aunt is prideful and resents being put in the position of having to apologize for taking sides and boycotting your wedding, then she needs to take that up with your mother. That's between the two of them, not you.

One caveat should you decide to spend Christmas with your mother- make sure you do it at *your* house. That's the only way to guarantee that no unpleasant surprises will be pulled on you, like your aunt and uncle just happening to "drop by" or your mother conspiring to arrange an impromptu reunion behind your back. Your reconciliation is too new and too precarious for you to be sure that your mother's loyalties now lie with you instead of her sister, and that she can be trusted to respect your wishes. Until you have had enough time to discern her spirit, choose the locations of your get-togethers carefully, so that *you* can control who shows up and who doesn't.

Preventive Medicine: The Wise Response To Someone Who Tries To Put You In The Middle

Many victims tend to suffer in silence, while it is their abusers who run around lying and trying to turn people against them so they will have no support system. Be aware that the person who comes to you and tries to involve you in her dispute with another adult, especially if this is someone you are not close enough to that you feel comfortable with such personal revelations, is most probably the actual abuser, playing the victim, lying about what happened, and trying to get you to gang up with her against the *real* victim. When you realize that you are being solicited as a Flying Monkey for an offender, and someone is trying to turn you against their target, you need to be prepared.

The first step is to differentiate between a dispute or simple discord and actual abuse or betrayal. We need to stay out of the feuds, arguments, and estrangements of other people. There is no reason at all for you to be involved in a disagreement or rift between two other adults. What is a proper mature response to a narcissistic relative who tries to drag you into a battle that has nothing to do with you? It's very simple: "I'm sorry you and Jasmine are having problems. I love you, but I love Jasmine, too. It makes me very uncomfortable that you seem to be trying to make me choose between you. I am not going to take sides in your disagreement, and I'd appreciate it if you don't try to put me in the middle. Thanks for understanding and I hope you can work things out." Period.

However, ongoing abuse, major betrayals and criminal behavior are a different story than mere quarrels, even quarrels in which the parties stop speaking to one another. If this is what is happening, our "neutrality" has the effect of supporting the abuser. In these cases, as people of integrity and good character, we need to make our disapproval clear. Unfortunately, there are going to be times when we will be put in the position of taking sides. For me, the choice is easy. God instructs us to have nothing to do with the wicked. So, when we have reason to believe someone is an abuser, narcissist or sociopath, we are not supposed to have anything further to do with him. If this is then interpreted to mean we have "taken sides" with the victim, so be it. We are *supposed to* take the side of those who are being victimized, wronged and downtrodden. If the rift involves actual abuse, it goes without saying that a decent, moral individual would support the target of that abuse and not, by refusing to "take sides," allow it to appear as if they approve of, condone or support the abuser in any way.

A Word To All The Abusers And Flying Monkeys Out There

As helpful as I pray this chapter might be for us Adult Children and other abuse survivors, there is a valuable lesson in here for you, too, if only you choose to take heed. It's well-known that the smear campaign is a typical weapon that abusers use against their victims. That being said, if you have had a disagreement or are not getting along with someone close to you, I hope and pray that you will think long and hard before you lie about, gossip or smear one family member to another, or pressure anyone else to take your side and outcast your child or whomever else you are currently feuding with. If, down the road, you should ever want to reconcile with your estranged relative, then how are you ever going to make it up to her for ruining her reputation and breaking up her relationships with other family members? Once you have caused others to think less of her, you will never be able to undo the damage you did. If everybody she cares about disowns her, then what possible motivation would she have for making up with *you* later on? If you are bent on "punishing" her, and succeed in taking everything away from her, then *she will have nothing left to lose* by locking you out of her life forever.

If you are a peripheral relative, barring actual abuse, crimes or betrayal, I hope you know better than to meddle in someone else's conflict, judge, take sides, add fuel to the fire, disown or "punish" anyone, betray someone who loves you and trusts you, or do anything other than *mind your own business and stay out of it.* If you managed to mind your own business and stay out of it all these years, standing by silently while one of your relatives mistreated another, then now that the family scapegoat is finally standing up for herself, it is not the time for you to finally open your mouth and jump into the fray- unless it's to defend the victim at last, and redeem yourself for all those years you looked the other way.

My advice to any judgmental friend or relative who doesn't have the maturity and self-control to keep their disapproval to themselves and understand that it is not their place to take sides in other people's petty arguments, is to think long and hard before you do something as major as boycotting a wedding, graduation party, or any other happy occasion for a family member who loves you and never did anything to hurt you. *These celebrations are once-in-a-lifetime events.* If you choose to takes sides and foolishly punish someone whom it is not your place to punish, by shunning or causing trouble on one of the biggest days of her life, *understand that you can never go back and undo it, and you will never be able to make up for it.* You will be shooting yourself in the foot and cutting off your own nose to spite your face.

Five or ten years down the road, when grandchildren marry, babies are born, or Uncle Snaggletooth dies, and the original enemies kiss and make up, loyalties will shift. The person you're siding with now, never a paragon of loyalty, honor and virtue to begin with, will be so anxious to stay on the good side of the person she just reconciled with that she will sell *you* out in a New York minute. And *you* will be the one whom nobody is speaking to!

The long-range ramifications of dragging other people into our battles, or allowing ourselves to be dragged into someone else's battles, can be quite daunting to repair once the damage has been done. Things can get very complicated and mushroom far beyond the control of those who think they can always go back and undo what they did anytime they want to. It's just not that simple, and many times it's not possible at all. Many disagreements between two people grow into family feuds and permanent estrangements that can never be fixed. This is especially true with betrayals.

Wise and mature people know this, which is why they refuse to allow others to involve them in conflicts that have nothing to do with them (again, barring actual abuse, criminal activity or treachery). The next time someone tries to drag you into a dispute that's none of your business, why not stop and think first, before you do something you might live to regret? Ask yourself what good it would do for you to disown your family member or friend based on the say-so of a third party. Try to do something *constructive,* instead of something even *more* destructive. Taking sides against someone who never did anything to you can mean that down the line, after everyone else has buried the hatchet, *you* will be the one on the outside looking in.

HE WHO GOES ABOUT AS A SLANDERER REVEALS SECRETS, THEREFORE DO NOT ASSOCIATE WITH A GOSSIP....Proverbs 20:19 NASB.

WHERE THERE IS NO WOOD, THE FIRE GOES OUT; AND WHERE THERE IS NO TALEBEARER STRIFE CEASES. AS CHARCOAL TO BURNING COALS, AND WOOD TO FIRE, SO IS A CONTENTIOUS MAN TO KINDLE STRIFE.... Proverbs 26:20-21 NKJV.

Chapter 17

The 3 Rs of Accountability: Repentance, Restitution, and Personal Responsibility

Being accountable for one's behavior is part of growing up and being a mature adult. It is also a necessary requirement for forgiveness. As we have seen, it is a fallacy that God is "all forgiving," in terms of the way that abusers interpret the word "all." When unrepentant offenders claim that "God forgives me," they are wrong. God does not forgive us until and unless we confess our sins and repent. The Lord holds us accountable for our behavior, and he instructs us to hold each other accountable as well.

Accountability consists of three elements: Repentance, Restitution, and Personal Responsibility:

Repentance
REPENTANCE: An earnest effort to make amends; contrition; remorse; turning from one's sinful ways; regret for past conduct resulting in a change of one's life; a sincere attempt to right a wrong one has committed and reverse its harmful effects; the forsaking of sin; atonement for a wrong including an admission of guilt, a promise not to repeat the

offense, and an attempt to make reparation; self-reproach, the abandonment of behavior which causes pain for others as a result of overwhelming feelings of shame for one's past actions.

When we rebuke, set limits on, or break off our relationship with an unrepentant offender, she may shrug and tell us, "Well, I know that *God* forgives me," the implication being that the Lord forgives her even if we don't. But guess what? She is *wrong*. The Lord *never* forgives unrepentant evildoers. He requires that sinners humble themselves and come to him for forgiveness, and that they show remorse and change their ways.

The Old Testament is full of examples of the Lord's wrath and punishment toward the Israelites every time they sinned against him and worshipped false idols, which they did repeatedly. Many times God lost his patience with them and they suffered the well-deserved consequences. He only forgave them when they asked for forgiveness (apologized), destroyed their false idols, and returned to worshipping him. In other words, when they *stopped* doing what offended him. The Lord does *not* forgive those who choose to continue sinning against him, and it is absurd to think that God requires more of us than he himself is willing to do. It is not possible for us to be more "godly" than God.

A mature adult is willing to be accountable for any distress or pain he has caused other people. A sincere apology, genuine remorse, and a determination to *stop* doing whatever is hurtful to others is known as repentance. Repentance is "forsaking sin" and "abandoning behavior that causes pain for others." It is not a mere apology. Repentance is constructive action. It is *change*.

Restitution
RESTITUTION: Reparation for injury or damage one has committed; compensation for loss; the act of making amends or making whole a person whom one has injured; returning

or restoring something of which a person has been unjustly deprived, or giving an equivalent; indemnification, making good, righting a wrong or injustice one has committed.

Restitution is an unfamiliar and often uncomfortable concept to many of us. It comes as quite a surprise to offenders to be told that they are expected to undo the damage they caused. It often comes as a surprise even to the victims, who for some reason don't really believe that they have the right to expect someone who did them wrong to fix what he did.

An important part of being accountable is making amends. Making amends includes *making it up to* the one who was hurt. It means undoing as much of the damage that you did as possible. It means making every effort to make the victim whole again- mentally, physically and emotionally - just like she was before the offender did whatever he did to her. It might include making her whole financially, by the offender paying back anything he borrowed, stole, or scammed the victim out of. It might include restoring the victim's reputation if he gossiped or lied about her- which would mean swallowing his pride, personally going to each person he gossiped or lied to, and setting the record straight. The idea is that the victim should not have to suffer the consequences of the abuser's actions. The abuser needs to be willing to suffer the consequences of his own actions, in order to make it right for the victim.

Some damage is so big that it seems irreversible, and indeed it might be. But there is always some restitution which the offender can offer. Something is better than nothing. If an offender has verbally, psychologically, emotionally, physically, or sexually abused a victim, she may have been so damaged by him that a way of making her whole does not easily present itself. There doesn't seem to be much an abuser could do to make it up to her. In such a case, restitution might consist of something like paying for the victim's therapy, or anything else he could do to respectfully admit, acknowledge, and alleviate the suffering he inflicted upon her.

The abuser can and should express a willingness to do whatever it takes to help the victim heal and recover. This would include offering to do anything the victim's therapist might suggest. The abuser might be asked to go to anger management or drug or alcohol rehab, enroll in an abuser program, or confess any crimes he committed against the victim to the police and go through the court/ prison system to pay his debt to her and to society. An essential component to properly making amends would be for the abuser to humbly allow the victim to express her pain and anger at him, to listen with respect, and to hear her out and validate her without becoming defensive or angry in return.

In the Bible, the Lord instructs us to make restitution to those we have wronged. The biblical model for restitution is returning what we have taken from another, and *adding to it* as well. In Leviticus, we are taught:

*THE LORD SAID TO MOSES: "IF ANYONE SINS AND IS UNFAITHFUL TO THE LORD BY DECEIVING HIS NEIGHBOR ABOUT SOMETHING ENTRUSTED TO HIM OR LEFT IN HIS CARE OR STOLEN, OR IF HE CHEATS HIM, OR IF HE FINDS LOST PROPERTY AND LIES ABOUT IT, OR IF HE SWEARS FALSELY, OR IF HE COMMITS ANY SUCH SIN THAT PEOPLE MAY DO- WHEN HE THUS SINS AND BECOMES GUILTY, HE MUST RETURN WHAT HE HAS STOLEN OR TAKEN BY EXTORTION, OR WHAT WAS ENTRUSTED TO HIM, OR THE LOST PROPERTY HE FOUND, OR WHATEVER IT WAS HE SWORE FALSELY ABOUT. **HE MUST MAKE RESTITUTION IN FULL, ADD A FIFTH OF THE VALUE TO IT**, AND GIVE IT ALL TO THE OWNER ON THE DAY HE PRESENTS HIS GUILT OFFERING. AND AS A PENALTY, HE MUST BRING TO THE PRIEST, THAT IS, TO THE LORD, HIS GUILT OFFERING.....AND HE WILL BE FORGIVEN FOR ANY OF THESE THINGS HE DID THAT MADE HIM GUILTY"...Leviticus 6:1-7 NIV.*

Notice also that this passage specifies restitution not just for theft of material goods, but for offenses such as *deception, swearing falsely, and any other such sins.*

This scripture illustrates yet another very important point. It is all too common for an offender to claim that since she has confessed her wrongdoing and repented to *God,* no further action on her part is required, especially when it comes to repenting to and making it up *to the victim.* But the Bible makes a distinction between repenting to God and repenting to the victim. *Both* are required for forgiveness, not just one. If one repents to God of one's sin *against God,* then God will forgive her. *But if an offender desires forgiveness for offenses against another person, then* **she must make amends to her victim** *in addition to repenting to God,* because she has offended both the Lord and her victim. We are told to first make restitution in full to the victim, including a penalty, and then to make an additional "guilt offering" to God. An offender who does not repent of her hurtful behavior *to the victim* is not entitled to anyone's forgiveness, including God's.

In Numbers, the Lord again makes it crystal clear that restitution, including interest, must be made *to the victim.* Only if the victim or his relatives cannot be found will restitution to the Lord alone be acceptable. Not being able to find the victim or his relatives does not let the perpetrator off the hook in terms of making restitution. He doesn't get to "keep what he took." He still has to pay the penalty for what he has done, except that in this case, all of it must be paid to the Lord. Again, note that restitution is expected for *any* wrong done to another person:

THE LORD SAID TO MOSES, "SAY TO THE ISRAELITES: **'WHEN A MAN OR WOMAN WRONGS ANOTHER IN ANY WAY** *AND SO IS UNFAITHFUL TO THE LORD, THAT PERSON IS GUILTY AND MUST CONFESS THE SIN HE HAS COMMITTED.* **HE MUST MAKE FULL RESTITUTION**

*FOR HIS WRONG, ADD ONE FIFTH TO IT AND GIVE
IT ALL TO THE PERSON HE HAS WRONGED. BUT IF
THAT PERSON HAS NO CLOSE RELATIVE TO WHOM
RESTITUTION CAN BE MADE FOR THE WRONG, THE
RESTITUTION BELONGS TO THE LORD AND MUST BE
GIVEN TO THE PRIEST, ALONG WITH THE RAM WITH
WHICH ATONEMENT IS MADE FOR HIM...Numbers
5:5-8 NIV.*

*IF A MAN SHALL STEAL AN OX, OR A SHEEP, AND KILL
IT, OR SELL IT;* **HE SHALL RESTORE FIVE OXEN FOR
AN OX, AND FOUR SHEEP FOR A SHEEP**.....*Exodus
22:1 KJV.*

A THIEF MUST CERTAINLY MAKE RESTITUTION,
*BUT IF HE HAS NOTHING, HE MUST BE SOLD TO PAY
FOR HIS THEFT. IF THE STOLEN ANIMAL IS FOUND
ALIVE IN HIS POSSESSION- WHETHER OX OR DONKEY
OR SHEEP-* **HE MUST PAY BACK DOUBLE**. *IF A MAN
GRAZES HIS LIVESTOCK IN A FIELD OR VINEYARD AND
THEY STRAY AND THEY GRAZE IN ANOTHER MAN'S
FIELD, HE* **MUST MAKE RESTITUTION** *FROM THE BEST
OF HIS OWN FIELD OR VINEYARD. IF A FIRE BREAKS
OUT AND SPREADS INTO THORNBUSHES SO THAT
IT BURNS SHOCKS OF GRAIN OR STANDING GRAIN
OR THE WHOLE FIELD, THE ONE WHO STARTED THE
FIRE* **MUST MAKE RESTITUTION**. *IF A MAN GIVES HIS
NEIGHBOR SILVER OR GOODS FOR SAFEKEEPING AND
THEY ARE STOLEN FROM THE NEIGHBOR'S HOUSE, THE
THIEF, IF HE IS CAUGHT,* **MUST PAY BACK DOUBLE**...
Exodus 22:3-7 NIV.

*.....BOTH PARTIES ARE TO BRING THEIR CASES BEFORE
THE JUDGES. THE ONE WHOM THE JUDGES DECLARE*

*GUILTY MUST **PAY BACK DOUBLE** TO HIS NEIGHBOR .....Exodus 22:9 NIV.*

*YET IF HE IS CAUGHT, HE **MUST PAY SEVENFOLD**, THOUGH IT COSTS HIM ALL THE WEALTH OF HIS HOUSE.....Proverbs 6:31 NIV.*

Many offenders have no understanding of, or simply don't care about, the pain their behavior causes for others. It's not even on their radar screens, as they just merrily go on wreaking havoc in other people's lives. Often the only way they can even begin to understand or empathize with their victims is to take the burden of their own actions back onto their own shoulders, and off the shoulders of their victims. Although it may not be easy and can be quite uncomfortable, an accountable adult will stand up and pay the price for what he did, instead of making another person pay the price. It's only right that an offender bear the consequences of his own actions, rather than someone else having to bear them.

Internalizing the idea that our actions do indeed have consequences may help an abuser to think twice before he hurts another innocent person. Having to undo the damage you've done is difficult, embarrassing, and humbling- and there are some things you will *never* be able to make up for. Learning to think first before you open your mouth or do something selfish or hurtful is a lesson well-learned, and making restitution for the wicked things you do is a great teacher.

God requires that restitution be made to victims by those who have victimized them. In specifying that an offender must *add extra* (one-fifth, double, sevenfold, etc.) to what they have taken, he requires those who have harmed others *to go above and beyond* in repairing the damage they've done. It is not enough to merely replace what was taken. The Lord expects an offender to make an additional sacrifice, and pay a penalty for what he did. Once again, we see that a mere apology is not sufficient. Making restitution is an important part of God's formula for forgiveness and the restoration of relationships. We need to *expect* those who have done us harm to undo the damage they have done, because that is what the Lord expects of them. If it is impossible to undo all of the damage, then we need to require them to undo as much as possible. God's justice is a perfect justice. He requires restitution, and so should we.

Personal Responsibility

RESPONSIBLE: Morally or legally obligated to take care of something; being to blame for something; liable; having to account for one's actions; being the cause of something harmful; obliged to remedy or prevent damage; reliable; trustworthy; answerable; honorable; accountable.

Personal responsibility means taking responsibility for yourself and your life. It includes such things as holding down a job, paying your own way, taking care of and protecting your children, being faithful and honorable, keeping promises and commitments, finishing what you've started, and being accountable for what you do and say. This is a character trait which normal, functioning adults develop as they mature. Of course, some mature much later than others. And some never mature at all.

Being responsible is what allows others to be able to trust you. When you are responsible, you are usually also trustworthy. Others know you will do the right thing. Responsible people are typically considered to be people of integrity and honor.

Accountable adults understand that they are responsible for their choices. They are responsible for the results of their decisions. They realize that if their words or actions cause something to happen, then they are responsible for what happened. And if they do harm, they are responsible for undoing it.

Many offenders are fond of saying, "But I didn't *mean* it that way," or, "I never meant for that to happen." *But intent is not the issue. Results are.*

Let's say you accidentally dropped hot coffee in your lap while driving, got distracted, ran a stop sign, and hit another car. You didn't *mean* to do it, but you did it anyway. There's no need to be defensive or view this as a personal attack- it's just a state-ment of fact. The accident is *your fault*, even though it was unin-tentional. That's the truth, plain and simple. You're the one who ran the stop sign, regardless of the reasons you had for doing it. It's certainly not the other driver's fault, because he had the right of way. So who should pay for the damage *you* did to his car? Or for the injuries *you* caused? Who should take responsibility? Who should be accountable? Certainly not the other guy- an innocent victim of *your* actions!

If you accidentally cause something to happen, *you still caused it.* If you unintentionally cause something to happen, *you still caused it.* If you inadvertently or carelessly cause something to happen, *you still caused it!* The damage is done, and the end result is the same, whether you meant it or not. And you still need to acknowledge that, and take responsibility for it. And if it wasn't an "accident," and you deliberately or selfishly caused pain for another person- well, shame on you. Then you're even *more* responsible for fixing what you did and making things right.

Everybody makes mistakes. Where most of us begin to lose our patience is with those who never *learn* from their "mistakes." This tells us that these are not really "mistakes" at all, but rather ongoing patterns of behavior. *A mistake is something you do unintentionally or accidentally.* Abuse is not unintentional. When an abuser repeats the same abusive behavior again and again, it is *not* "a mistake." He didn't do it "by accident." If something is truly accidental or inadvertent, an accountable adult will have no problem sincerely apologizing, doing whatever he can to fix the situation, and moving on. Mature adults do not have a problem apologizing for errors in judgment, or innocent mistakes that caused harm to others. There is no guilt or shame attached to a truly unintentional offense.

Only those who feel guilty or ashamed will avoid taking responsibility for the things they've done. One who did wrong deliberately, selfishly, or with malicious intent will be ashamed when she is caught or confronted, so she will not admit what she did. She will try to hide it, make excuses, or in some way weasel out of being accountable for her behavior. She will be angry and flustered at being caught, when she thought she was getting away with it. She will not admit she was wrong, she will not sincerely apologize, and she will not try to rectify the damage she caused.

The reason that guilt or shame is felt is that, despite what the offender might say, her words or actions *were intentional*. Or, at the very least, *selfish*. One way or the other, she knew what she was doing and the effects it might have. But she decided to do it anyway, and hope for the best. Otherwise she would have nothing to be ashamed of and no problem acting in a responsible manner and making amends. Her ego would not be at stake, and she would not react with the shame of someone who was "caught" doing wrong. One who feels guilty or ashamed will lie, deny, cover-up, blame others- anything but admit that she was wrong and take responsibility for her own words and actions.

On the other hand, someone who is not ashamed of herself has no reason to deny or lie about what she did. She will acknowledge her actions, apologize for the pain she caused *even though she didn't mean to*, admit that she was wrong, used poor judgment, or made a mistake, do everything she can to make restitution, and *not repeat* the same offense in the future. She may feel embarrassed about her actions, but she will not feel the shame that leads to covering them up. And she understands that failure to take responsibility would be an even greater reason to be embarrassed.

When you demonstrate personal responsibility, you are living up to what is expected of you by your friends and family, society, yourself, and the Lord. You are acting in a righteous manner. Being accountable means being honorable. It means that people can depend on you and rely on you. It means that others can trust you. It means you have integrity. It means that you will do whatever is necessary to right a wrong- and that includes repentance and restitution. *Accountable* people are people who can be *counted on*. When we repent of our wrongdoing, make amends and restitution to the people we have hurt by undoing as much of the damage we have done as possible, and take personal responsibility for our words and behavior and their results, then we teach others that we are a person of integrity- an honorable, trustworthy, mature adult. This is what being accountable is all about.

> *IF YOU RETURN TO THE ALMIGHTY, YOU WILL BE RESTORED; IF YOU REMOVE WICKEDNESS FAR FROM YOUR TENT.....Job 22:23 NIV.*

> *FOR IF YOU THROUGHLY AMEND YOUR WAYS AND YOUR DOINGS; IF YOU THROUGHLY EXECUTE JUDGMENT BETWEEN A MAN AND HIS NEIGHBOUR .....THEN I WILL CAUSE YOU TO DWELL IN THIS PLACE, IN THE LAND THAT I GAVE TO YOUR FATHERS, FOR EVER AND EVER......Jeremiah 7:5,7 KJV.*

Chapter 18

How Can I Forgive?

Before we embark on the journey to forgiveness, it helps to define what forgiveness means to us, and to put the offense against us into perspective as well. Forgiveness can be defined as *ceasing to feel resentment*. It's important to understand that we should never force forgiveness prematurely. We need not even make a conscious effort to forgive. We only need to reach the point of being willing to let it go, and let the Lord work on our hearts. Time and God's grace has a way of lessening the hurt and erasing the resentment. We are not going to still be angry ten or twenty years down the road. One way of looking at forgiveness is to let time and God heal the wounds, until we just don't care anymore. We have no more anger, no more hurt, no more need to see justice done. We don't wish anything bad or anything good for our ex-abusers, we don't wish anything at all. We no longer feel resentment toward the one who harmed us because we no longer feel *anything* toward her, and that's fine.

The path to forgiveness involves analyzing, understanding, and internalizing three main concepts:

1. **Forgiveness has nothing to do with reconciliation.** We are often actually *afraid* to forgive, because we believe that forgiveness means we must "make up with" our abuser and expose ourselves to more abuse or trigger our PTSD just by being in her presence. Our abusers and their Flying Monkeys tend to assume that if we forgive them, it automatically means that we will also reconcile the relationship, and things will "go back to normal." Many times, even *we* fail to recognize that "forgiveness" and "reconciliation" are not the same thing. These two words have obviously different meanings and do not necessarily go together, any more than "forgive" and "forget" necessarily go hand-in-hand.

There is no requirement to reconcile a relationship with someone who has harmed you in the past. It is strictly up to you. In deciding whether or not to reconcile when we forgive, we need to consider several aspects concerning the offenses committed against us:

Intent:

The disciples Judas Iscariot and Simon Peter both betrayed Jesus. Besides that Judas' betrayal resulted in Jesus' death (which was necessary to fulfill the prophesies in Scripture and for the salvation of mankind), why was Judas eternally damned for his betrayal, while Peter was forgiven, completely reconciled to Jesus, and trusted by Jesus to take care of his people (John 21:15-25)? Because Peter impulsively betrayed Jesus out of fear, while Judas *intentionally* plotted and planned to betray Jesus out of greed and his own selfish motivations. Judas knew that his betrayal would have devastating consequences for Jesus, *but he didn't care!*

We might consider reconciling with someone who thoughtlessly hurt us, not realizing that their actions or words would be harmful. But we should be very wary of reconciling with someone who *knew* that we would be hurt and did it anyway.

Magnitude & Frequency:

One or two nasty remarks do not constitute a pattern of abuse. If someone has an occasional lapse in judgment or temper that results in our feelings being hurt, I believe such slip-ups are common in most relationships and we should try to overlook it. However, if the behavior is an *ongoing pattern*, or our friend or relative has stabbed us in the back or been emotionally, mentally, physically, or sexually abusive toward us, then we *must* protect ourselves. And certainly, if we have children, it is our duty as a parent to protect them from experiencing or witnessing abuse as well.

When do hurt feelings and insults cross the line into abuse? When they become a continual, recurring pattern, a repetitive way of relating to you, or when they begin to undermine your self-esteem, cause you stress, or impact your health.

Besides the frequency of the misbehavior, the *magnitude* of it needs to be considered as well. An insult is not on the same level as a serious betrayal where trust has been broken, possibly beyond repair. If your sister hurt your feelings by criticizing your new hairstyle, you are probably not going to feel as unforgiving toward her as you would if she slept with your husband. Someone who accidentally forgot your birthday is not necessarily evil; whereas someone who stole your identity, took your money and ruined your credit, is. Someone who kept you waiting half an hour for a date might be inconsiderate, but not wicked. However, there is little doubt that someone who gossiped and lied about you, tried to ruin your reputation and turn other people against you, is wicked. Someone who is occasionally rude or impatient with you but basically loving and polite would not be considered downright evil, whereas someone who has spent the last twenty or thirty years browbeating, manipulating, and gaslighting you, would be. These are all things you need to consider that will have an effect on your ability to forgive, and certainly on your willingness to reconcile. Small, inadvertent and uncharacteristic offenses by people who do not have malicious intentions are the ones the Lord wants us to be quick to forgive, or more accurately, slow to become angry over:

WHEREFORE, MY BELOVED BRETHREN, LET EVERY MAN BE SWIFT TO HEAR, SLOW TO SPEAK, SLOW TO WRATH…James 1:19 KJV.

Big offenses, treachery, criminal and quasi-criminal behavior and abuse, on the other hand, are usually committed by those who are biblically defined as evil. They require a lot more effort than a mere apology on the part of the offender to merit forgiveness, and reconciliation may very well be out of the question. Unless the wicked one proves over time that he has truly repented and turned his life over to God, he remains evil, and the Lord has instructed us to have nothing to do with the evil.

Repentance:

When you rebuke someone who has sinned against you, if she loves you, cares for you, and truly didn't mean any harm, her first response will be to apologize. And her second response will be to make a commitment to never do it again. Abusive people, of course, will not react in this way. A wicked person may very well apologize, but it will not be from her heart and will not be sincere. She is not sorry for hurting you. She is only sorry that she was caught and called on it! Her apology, if there is one, will be self-serving, calculated to get you to drop the subject or to deceive you into believing that she has changed. In truth, she has no intentions of changing her ways, and no desire to. In many cases, only time will tell if a person is truly repentant and you can trust her enough to think about the possibility of a reconciliation.

After considering these aspects, we must understand that *we can forgive and still protect ourselves.* God does not expect us to continue exposing ourselves and our loved ones to evil or to someone we can't trust. We have a divine right to protect ourselves and a divine responsibility to protect our spouses and our children from abuse or treachery and its effects. Note the following instructions which pertain to "brothers" in Christ. If the Lord tells us to shun a divisive brother in the church, how much *more* (not less) would these instructions logically apply to one who is not a fellow believer:

> IF ANYONE IS CAUSING DIVISIONS AMONG YOU, GIVE A FIRST AND SECOND WARNING. AFTER THAT, **HAVE NOTHING MORE TO DO WITH THAT PERSON** ....Titus 3:10 NLT.

> I URGE YOU, BROTHERS, TO WATCH OUT FOR THOSE WHO CAUSE DIVISIONS AND PUT OBSTACLES IN YOUR WAY THAT ARE CONTRARY TO THE TEACHING YOU HAVE LEARNED. **KEEP AWAY FROM THEM**. FOR SUCH PEOPLE ARE NOT SERVING OUR LORD CHRIST, BUT THEIR OWN APPETITES. BY SMOOTH TALK AND FLATTERY THEY DECEIVE THE MINDS OF NAÏVE PEOPLE.....Romans 16:17-18 NIV.

2. **There is no deadline for forgiveness, and no reason to rush into it before we are ready.** Although the eventual goal might be forgiveness, there is no set timetable. Forgiveness is not something we need to do immediately or give on demand, and in many cases that will not even be mentally or emotionally possible. In order to completely forgive, first we need an understanding of what it is we're forgiving. This means taking the time to process our hurt, feel our anger, and grieve the way we have been treated by people we love. Therapy can be very helpful, but even without therapy, as you start to process your grief and anger, you are likely to start remembering many other long-forgotten abuses, which you will then, in turn, need time to process. This is a necessary step on the road to healing.

While forgiving means ceasing to feel resentment, it does not mean that we "forget," cease to talk about, or cover up what was done to us. We are scripturally ordained to rebuke and admonish those who do evil. We must not protect them by our silence. We are to talk about evil deeds and bring them into the light (Matthew 10:26-27; John 3:19-21).

Knowing that their words and actions will not remain hidden will make many abusers think twice before victimizing someone again. It is our responsibility to speak the truth (John 8:32). We must never, by failure to speak up, give the impression that we condone or approve of evil acts. We need to reach a point where we can forgive without denying or hiding the truth of what was done to us, and that will take time.

3. **Pray.** Prayer is the secret to healing our pain and being able to forgive. Of course, we must pray for the courage and the peace to forgive. We need the comfort of the Holy Spirit. We need grace from our Savior Jesus. And we need to be anchored in the love of our real Father.

Now I am going to reveal to you the true secret of forgiveness: *Pray for the person who hurt you!*

In addition to praying for all the nice, loving, caring people in our lives, try praying for those who choose to be our enemies. Pray that their hard hearts will be softened, that their eyes will be unveiled, that their minds will be opened, and that they will see the error of their ways and repent.

Above all, pray for their salvation. This is very hard at first, and you may not feel as if you are being sincere. But it will get easier after a while. It is difficult to continue to feel unable to forgive someone you pray for. Eventually, you will begin to feel more open to forgiving that person if the day ever comes that he changes his evil ways and makes proper amends. Forgiveness, if it has been earned by repentance, will help *us* to leave the past behind, move on, and live the rich and full lives God intended for us.

BUT I SAY, LOVE YOUR ENEMIES! PRAY FOR THOSE WHO PERSECUTE YOU! IN THAT WAY, YOU WILL BE ACTING AS TRUE CHILDREN OF YOUR FATHER IN HEAVEN...... Matthew 5:44-45 NLT.

BLESS THOSE WHO CURSE YOU, PRAY FOR THOSE WHO MISTREAT YOU.....Luke 6:28 NASB.

Praying for the one who hurt us is key. Remember, you can pray for her just fine from a safe distance. You do not have to see her or speak to her ever again, but you can still pray when you feel ready to. It's also okay if that's years down the road. Whenever you feel ready, you can do it.

Chapter 19

Do I Have to Let Anyone Know When I Have Forgiven?

Over the years, I have come to realize that there are a couple of big misconceptions about forgiveness. It's important for survivors to understand exactly what forgiveness entails and does not entail, so they can continue to protect themselves and their loved ones from the possibility of more abuse or treachery.

First, *there is no biblical requirement that you must let someone know in person when you forgive him.* You can forgive in your heart, from a safe distance, and without personal contact. Unless you are interested in reconciling the relationship, or she has repented and knowing you forgive her is important to her, there is no need to make a point of telling your ex-abuser. Telling someone who hasn't even asked for forgiveness that you forgive him anyway is just asking for more trouble.

And second, the Bible does not tell you to show or tell *other people* that you have forgiven. Trying to prove your righteousness to other people by making sure they know you have forgiven is prideful- and pride is a sin. As a Christian, you are not supposed to boast about how good you are. You are supposed to be humble and keep the "good" things you do to yourself. Forgiveness has nothing to do with any third parties and is none of their business. Keeping Flying Monkeys in the loop also tends to reinforce their belief that they have a right to know what you're thinking or doing and that you must always try to earn their approval. While many of us at least understand that forgiveness is between you and the offender and not any third parties, we can take that one step further and say that *in reality whether or not you have forgiven is only between you and God.* You do not need witnesses. God is your witness.

You have no obligation to forgive an unrepentant evildoer, even on his deathbed. You are not supposed to force yourself on unrepentant people who do not welcome your overtures.

And if you do forgive him, it is perfectly okay to do it in your heart without announcing it to the whole family or group. This is your own private spiritual work. You don't have to let your ex-abuser or anyone else know for it to count.

Chapter 20

WWJRD? What Would Jesus *Really* Do?

Why is it that when we ask ourselves, "What would Jesus do?" the Jesus that almost always comes to mind is the Jesus whom we have read about in the gospels of the apostles? And then, why do we go on to misinterpret what the gospels reveal about our Lord's nature, by seeing him only as endlessly forgiving and patient with everyone, and so meek and mild that he placidly allowed himself to be dragged away to his own death, and somehow forgetting all the times he boldly confronted the wicked?

Allow me to pose this question: When we ask ourselves, "What would Jesus do?", why do we never think of Jesus as depicted in The Book of Revelation- a great and mighty warrior, righteous and just, awesome and powerful, who will gather his saints to him to live in paradise, and throw everything evil- men and women, demons and devils- into the lake of fire for all eternity?

One problem seems to be that many of us don't read Revelation. It is sometimes difficult to understand, but much of this can be overcome by reading and comparing the different versions of the Bible, using a study guide, and praying for understanding from the Holy Ghost, who will open our eyes and make all scripture accessible to us.

Some folks readily admit that they don't read Revelation, because, quite frankly, it scares them. I truly believe this is one of the biggest reasons why many of us feel reluctant to study this book. Let's face it, reading about the end of the world and Armageddon certainly sounds terrifying. It seems that few of us stick it out long enough to get through the "scary stuff" and read Revelation's magnificent and glorious ending. All fears and sorrows will be gone. Our joy will be unsurpassed in that day! Praise and glory to our Lord and God!

> I WAS IN THE SPIRIT ON THE LORD'S DAY, AND I HEARD BEHIND ME A LOUD VOICE, AS OF A TRUMPET, SAYING "I AM THE ALPHA AND THE OMEGA, THE FIRST AND THE LAST"....THEN I TURNED TO SEE THE VOICE THAT SPOKE WITH ME. AND HAVING TURNED I SAW SEVEN GOLDEN LAMPSTANDS, AND IN THE MIDST OF THE SEVEN LAMPSTANDS ONE LIKE THE SON OF MAN, CLOTHED WITH A GARMENT DOWN TO THE FEET AND GIRDED ABOUT THE CHEST WITH A GOLDEN BAND. HIS HEAD AND HAIR WERE WHITE LIKE WOOL, AS WHITE AS SNOW, AND HIS EYES LIKE A FLAME OF FIRE; HIS FEET WERE LIKE FINE BRASS, AS IF REFINED IN A FURNACE, AND HIS VOICE AS THE SOUND OF MANY WATERS; HE HAD IN HIS RIGHT HAND SEVEN STARS, OUT OF HIS MOUTH WENT A SHARP TWO-EDGED SWORD, AND HIS COUNTENANCE WAS LIKE THE SUN SHINING IN ITS STRENGTH. AND WHEN I SAW HIM, I FELL AT HIS FEET AS DEAD. BUT HE LAID HIS RIGHT HAND ON ME, SAYING TO ME, "DO NOT BE AFRAID; I AM THE FIRST AND THE LAST. I AM HE WHO LIVES, AND WAS DEAD, AND BEHOLD, I AM ALIVE FOREVERMORE. AMEN. AND I HAVE THE KEYS OF HADES AND OF DEATH" ....Revelation 1:10-18 NKJV.

Hmmm, so far, Jesus is not sounding so meek and mild. But he is also telling us not to be afraid! Thank you, Lord.

"WE GIVE YOU THANKS, O LORD GOD ALMIGHTY, THE ONE WHO IS AND WHO WAS AND WHO IS TO COME, BECAUSE YOU HAVE TAKEN YOUR GREAT POWER AND REIGNED. THE NATIONS WERE ANGRY, AND YOUR WRATH HAS COME, AND THE TIME OF THE DEAD, THAT THEY SHOULD BE JUDGED, AND THAT YOU SHOULD REWARD YOUR SERVANTS THE PROPHETS AND THE SAINTS, AND THOSE WHO FEAR YOUR NAME, SMALL AND GREAT, AND SHOULD DESTROY THOSE WHO DESTROY THE EARTH"....Revelation 11:17-18 NKJV.

AND I HEARD ANOTHER VOICE FROM HEAVEN SAYING, "COME OUT OF HER, MY PEOPLE, LEST YOU SHARE IN HER SINS, AND LEST YOU RECEIVE OF HER PLAGUES. FOR HER SINS HAVE REACHED TO HEAVEN, AND GOD HAS REMEMBERED HER INIQUITIES. RENDER TO HER JUST AS SHE RENDERED TO YOU, AND REPAY HER DOUBLE ACCORDING TO HER WORKS; IN THE CUP WHICH SHE HAS MIXED, MIX DOUBLE FOR HER. IN THE MEASURE THAT SHE GLORIFIED HERSELF AND LIVED LUXURIOUSLY, IN THE SAME MEASURE GIVE HER TORMENT AND SORROW; FOR SHE SAYS IN HER HEART, 'I SIT AS QUEEN, AND AM NO WIDOW, AND WILL NOT SEE SORROW.' THEREFORE HER PLAGUES WILL COME IN ONE DAY- DEATH AND MOURNING AND FAMINE. AND SHE WILL BE UTTERLY BURNED WITH FIRE, FOR STRONG IS THE LORD GOD WHO JUDGES HER. THE KINGS OF THE EARTH WHO COMMITTED FORNICATION AND LIVED LUXURIOUSLY WITH HER WILL WEEP AND LAMENT FOR HER, WHEN THEY SEE THE SMOKE OF

HER BURNING, STANDING AT A DISTANCE FOR FEAR OF HER TORMENT, SAYING, 'ALAS, ALAS, THAT GREAT CITY BABYLON, THAT MIGHTY CITY! FOR IN ONE HOUR YOUR JUDGMENT HAS COME'"....Revelation 18:4-10 NKJV.

And so we learn that Jesus is not endlessly forgiving and patient, and he most certainly is not forgiving and patient where evil and wickedness are concerned. *Jesus does not forgive everyone.* Those who do not repent, accept Jesus as their Lord, and change their evil ways, will never be forgiven, not even at the end of time:

AND I SAW A GREAT WHITE THRONE, AND HIM THAT SAT ON IT, FROM WHOSE FACE THE EARTH AND THE HEAVEN FLED AWAY; AND THERE WAS FOUND NO PLACE FOR THEM. AND I SAW THE DEAD, SMALL AND GREAT, STAND BEFORE GOD; AND THE BOOKS WERE OPENED: AND ANOTHER BOOK WAS OPENED, WHICH IS THE BOOK OF LIFE: AND THE DEAD WERE JUDGED OUT OF THOSE THINGS WHICH WERE WRITTEN IN THE BOOKS, ACCORDING TO THEIR WORKS. AND THE SEA GAVE UP THE DEAD WHICH WERE IN IT; AND DEATH AND HELL DELIVERED UP THE DEAD WHICH WERE IN THEM: AND THEY WERE JUDGED EVERY MAN ACCORDING TO THEIR WORKS. AND DEATH AND HELL WERE CAST INTO THE LAKE OF FIRE. THIS IS THE SECOND DEATH. AND WHOSOEVER WAS NOT FOUND WRITTEN IN THE BOOK OF LIFE WAS CAST INTO THE LAKE OF FIRE.

AND I SAW A NEW HEAVEN AND A NEW EARTH: FOR THE FIRST HEAVEN AND THE FIRST EARTH WERE PASSED AWAY; AND THERE WAS NO MORE SEA. AND I JOHN SAW THE HOLY CITY, NEW JERUSALEM, COMING

DOWN FROM GOD OUT OF HEAVEN, PREPARED AS A BRIDE ADORNED FOR HER HUSBAND. AND I HEARD A GREAT VOICE OUT OF HEAVEN SAYING, BEHOLD, THE TABERNACLE OF GOD IS WITH MEN, AND HE WILL DWELL WITH THEM, AND THEY SHALL BE HIS PEOPLE, AND GOD HIMSELF SHALL BE WITH THEM, AND BE THEIR GOD. AND GOD SHALL WIPE AWAY ALL TEARS FROM THEIR EYES; AND THERE SHALL BE NO MORE DEATH, NEITHER SORROW, NOR CRYING, NEITHER SHALL THERE BE ANY MORE PAIN: FOR THE FORMER THINGS ARE PASSED AWAY. AND HE THAT SAT UPON THE THRONE SAID, BEHOLD, I MAKE ALL THINGS NEW. AND HE SAID UNTO ME, WRITE: FOR THESE WORDS ARE TRUE AND FAITHFUL. AND HE SAID UNTO ME, IT IS DONE. I AM ALPHA AND OMEGA, THE BEGINNING AND THE END. I WILL GIVE UNTO HIM THAT IS ATHIRST OF THE FOUNTAIN OF THE WATER OF LIFE FREELY. HE THAT OVERCOMETH SHALL INHERIT ALL THINGS, AND I WILL BE HIS GOD, AND HE SHALL BE MY SON. BUT THE FEARFUL, AND UNBELIEVING, AND THE ABOMINABLE, AND MURDERERS, AND WHOREMONGERS, AND SORCERERS, AND IDOLATERS, AND ALL LIARS, SHALL HAVE THEIR PART IN THE LAKE WHICH BURNETH WITH FIRE AND BRIMSTONE: WHICH IS THE SECOND DEATH.....Revelation 20:11- 21:8 KJV.

When we think of Jesus, many of us picture a passive, meek, gentle man. In some of our minds, Jesus was the first hippie, believing in peace at all costs. We see him as being placid, unassuming, low-key, complacent, and serene, even in the face of interrogation, false accusations, torture, suffering, and death.

But this is a huge misconception. Revelation certainly does not support this perception of Jesus' nature, and neither do the gospels. Jesus was indeed kind and gentle when it was called for and to those who merited such treatment. But we should not mistake his kindness or gentleness for weakness. Jesus was not, and is not, some wishy-washy milquetoast who lets everybody do whatever they want and never speaks up. He is the King of Kings, and he acts like the King of Kings! The biblical Jesus was at all times in control and in command of what was going on around him. He is Master, Teacher, Rabbi. How could he possibly teach us right from wrong if all he did was keep silent when someone was doing something wrong?

Selective memory may be a factor in this misunderstanding of Jesus' character and temperament. It seems as if none of us have a problem recalling the compassion, mercy, kindness and love that Jesus had for the poor, the weak, the suffering, the children, the humble, the sorrowful, the widows and the orphans. But for some reason we tend to forget the firm stand he always took against wickedness. I can't picture Jesus casting out a demon by politely asking it to please leave- nothing personal and no offense intended, just please go, if you don't mind! That is not at all how Jesus dealt with evil. From rebuking and harsh words for sinners and evildoers to driving out demons, Jesus was far from patient, meek, tolerant, or laid-back. He was mighty and powerful, and he always took a firm and decisive stand against all evil behavior:

AND HE WENT INTO THE TEMPLE, AND BEGAN TO CAST OUT THEM THAT SOLD THEREIN, AND THEM THAT BOUGHT; SAYING UNTO THEM, IT IS WRITTEN, MY HOUSE IS THE HOUSE OF PRAYER, BUT YE HAVE MADE IT A DEN OF THIEVES....Luke 19:45-46 KJV.

WHY DO YE NOT UNDERSTAND MY SPEECH? EVEN BECAUSE YE CANNOT HEAR MY WORD. YE ARE OF YOUR FATHER THE DEVIL, AND THE LUSTS OF YOUR FATHER YE WILL DO. HE WAS A MURDERER FROM THE BEGINNING, AND ABODE NOT IN THE TRUTH, BECAUSE

THERE IS NO TRUTH IN HIM. WHEN HE SPEAKETH A LIE, HE SPEAKETH OF HIS OWN: FOR HE IS A LIAR, AND THE FATHER OF IT. AND BECAUSE I TELL YOU THE TRUTH, YE BELIEVE ME NOT. WHICH OF YOU CONVINCETH ME OF SIN? AND IF I SAY THE TRUTH, WHY DO YE NOT BELIEVE ME? HE THAT IS OF GOD HEARETH GOD'S WORDS: YE THEREFORE HEAR THEM NOT, BECAUSE YE ARE NOT OF GOD....John 8:43-47 KJV.

Jesus did not wrack his brain trying to think of pleasant little euphemisms for unacceptable behavior that wouldn't insult the offenders or hurt their feelings. He did not try to "choose his words" or "approach them carefully," so they wouldn't think he was attacking them or accusing them of doing wrong. In fact, if they did wrong, he accused them of it point-blank, and publicly. He was tough and direct. He did not negotiate. He showed no inclination whatsoever to "compromise" with evil, or to "find a solution that everyone can be happy with." Jesus had no problem coming right out and calling a liar a liar:

THOUGH YOU DO NOT KNOW HIM, I KNOW HIM. IF I SAID I DID NOT, I WOULD BE A LIAR LIKE YOU, BUT I DO KNOW HIM AND KEEP HIS WORD....John 8:55 NIV.

Jesus was, and is, *God*. And during the time he walked among us, *he acted like God!* Can you imagine God standing by and silently watching abuse? Can you imagine God walking on eggshells to avoid offending an abuser? He was our Savior, and he acted like a Savior. He was our Teacher, and he taught us. He spoke the truth no matter what the opposition might be. He was righteous and just. Jesus did not pussyfoot around evildoers, no matter how powerful they were. He exposed them. He never protected them with his silence or covered up for them- and he admonished us not to, either. He did not look the other way and ignore unacceptable behavior in order to "keep the peace." He instructed us to bring evil deeds into the light and expose them. Jesus was outspoken, firm, and strong. He did not mince words, and he called a spade a spade:

JESUS SAID, "YOU'RE RIGHT! YOU DON'T HAVE A HUSBAND- FOR YOU HAVE HAD FIVE HUSBANDS, AND YOU AREN'T EVEN MARRIED TO THE MAN YOU'RE LIVING WITH NOW"....John 4:17 NLT.

I CAME TO SEND FIRE ON THE EARTH, AND HOW I WISH IT WERE ALREADY KINDLED! BUT I HAVE A BAPTISM TO BE BAPTIZED WITH, AND HOW DISTRESSED I AM TILL IT IS ACCOMPLISHED! DO YOU SUPPOSE THAT I CAME TO GIVE PEACE ON EARTH? I TELL YOU, NOT AT ALL, BUT RATHER DIVISION. FOR FROM NOW ON FIVE IN ONE HOUSE WILL BE DIVIDED: THREE AGAINST TWO AND TWO AGAINST THREE. FATHER WILL BE DIVIDED AGAINST SON AND SON AGAINST FATHER, MOTHER AGAINST DAUGHTER AND DAUGHTER AGAINST MOTHER, MOTHER-IN-LAW AGAINST HER DAUGHTER-IN-LAW AND DAUGHTER-IN-LAW AGAINST HER MOTHER-IN-LAW.....Luke 12:49-53 NKJV.

*SO DO NOT BE AFRAID OF THEM. THERE IS NOTHING CONCEALED THAT WILL NOT BE DISCLOSED, OR HIDDEN THAT WILL NOT BE MADE KNOWN. WHAT I TELL YOU IN THE DARK, SPEAK IN THE DAYLIGHT: **WHAT IS WHISPERED IN YOUR EAR, PROCLAIM FROM THE ROOFS**....Matthew 10:26-27 NIV.*

*BEWARE OF THE LEAVEN OF THE PHARISEES, WHICH IS HYPOCRISY. BUT **THERE IS NOTHING COVERED UP THAT WILL NOT BE REVEALED, AND HIDDEN THAT***

WILL NOT BE KNOWN. ACCORDINGLY, WHATEVER YOU HAVE SAID IN THE DARK WILL BE HEARD IN THE LIGHT, AND WHAT YOU HAVE WHISPERED IN THE INNER ROOMS WILL BE PROCLAIMED UPON THE HOUSETOPS....Luke 12:1-3 NASB.

*DO NOT THINK THAT I CAME TO BRING PEACE ON EARTH. **I DID NOT COME TO BRING PEACE BUT A SWORD.** FOR I HAVE COME TO "SET A MAN AGAINST HIS FATHER, A DAUGHTER AGAINST HER MOTHER, AND A DAUGHTER-IN-LAW AGAINST HER MOTHER-IN-LAW"; AND "A MAN'S ENEMIES WILL BE THOSE OF HIS OWN HOUSEHOLD." HE WHO LOVES FATHER OR MOTHER MORE THAN ME IS NOT WORTHY OF ME. AND HE WHO LOVES SON OR DAUGHTER MORE THAN ME IS NOT WORTHY OF ME. AND HE WHO DOES NOT TAKE HIS CROSS AND FOLLOW AFTER ME IS NOT WORTHY OF ME. HE WHO FINDS HIS LIFE WILL LOSE IT, AND HE WHO LOSES HIS LIFE FOR MY SAKE WILL FIND IT....Matthew 10:34-39 NKJV.*

As believers, we try our best to model our own behavior after our Lord's. We want to be "Christ-like." When faced with wrongdoing, bad behavior, and wicked people, some of us ask ourselves "What would Jesus do?" And then we use what we imagine would be Jesus' reaction to justify being "tolerant" or "patient" with evildoers who consistently cause pain for ourselves and others. Sometimes we tolerate abuse because we think we are the only target and we "can take it." But that is seldom the case. Most abusers target other victims, too- not just us. That is their pattern of behavior, and we owe it to ourselves, as well as the other innocent victims, to take a stand.

Jesus was never tolerant or patient with those who did wrong. We might imagine that Jesus always tried to "keep the peace," but that is not true at all. Jesus never backed away from a conflict. He did not hesitate to rebuke a sinner. He himself instructs us to rebuke wrongdoers. Jesus makes a point of telling us to forgive *if there is repentance* (Luke 17:3). He never tells us to be endlessly patient with abusers, or to stick around for more abuse. Instead, as we have learned, he clearly tells us to avoid and shun those who continue in their bad behavior and who refuse to listen to our rebuke:

*THEREFORE BY THEIR FRUITS YOU WILL KNOW THEM. NOT EVERYONE WHO SAYS TO ME, "LORD, LORD," SHALL ENTER THE KINGDOM OF HEAVEN, BUT HE WHO DOES THE WILL OF MY FATHER IN HEAVEN. MANY WILL SAY TO ME IN THAT DAY, "LORD, LORD, HAVE WE NOT PROPHESIED IN YOUR NAME, CAST OUT DEMONS IN YOUR NAME, AND DONE MANY WONDERS IN YOUR NAME?" AND THEN I WILL DECLARE TO THEM, "**I NEVER KNEW YOU; DEPART FROM ME, YOU WHO PRACTICE LAWLESSNESS!**"....Matthew 7:20-23 NKJV.*

*IF THE HOUSEHOLD IS WORTHY, LET YOUR PEACE COME UPON IT. BUT IF IT IS NOT WORTHY, LET YOUR PEACE RETURN TO YOU. AND WHOEVER WILL NOT RECEIVE YOU NOR HEAR YOUR WORDS, **WHEN YOU DEPART FROM THAT HOUSE OR CITY, SHAKE OFF THE DUST FROM YOUR FEET.** ASSUREDLY, I SAY TO YOU, IT WILL BE MORE TOLERABLE FOR THE LAND OF SODOM AND GOMORRAH IN THE DAY OF JUDGMENT THAT FOR THAT CITY! BEHOLD, I SEND YOU OUT AS SHEEP IN THE MIDST OF WOLVES. THEREFORE BE WISE AS SERPENTS AND HARMLESS AS DOVES....Matthew 10:13-16 NKJV.*

*AND WHOEVER WILL NOT RECEIVE YOU NOR HEAR YOU, WHEN YOU DEPART FROM THERE, **SHAKE OFF***

THE DUST UNDER YOUR FEET AS A TESTIMONY AGAINST THEM....*Mark 6:11 NKJV.*

*IF YOUR BROTHER SINS AGAINST YOU, **GO AND SHOW HIM HIS FAULT**, JUST BETWEEN THE TWO OF YOU. IF HE LISTENS TO YOU, YOU HAVE WON YOUR BROTHER OVER. BUT IF HE WILL NOT LISTEN, TAKE ONE OR TWO OTHERS ALONG, SO THAT 'EVERY MATTER MAY BE ESTABLISHED BY THE TESTIMONY OF TWO OR THREE WITNESSES.' IF HE REFUSES TO LISTEN TO THEM, TELL IT TO THE CHURCH; AND IF HE REFUSES TO LISTEN EVEN TO THE CHURCH, **TREAT HIM AS YOU WOULD A PAGAN OR A TAX COLLECTOR**....Matthew 18:15-17 NIV.*

Jesus did not hesitate to rebuke even his own apostles:

*HAVE NOT I CHOSEN YOU TWELVE, AND **ONE OF YOU IS A DEVIL?** HE SPAKE OF JUDAS ISCARIOT THE SON OF SIMON: FOR HE IT WAS THAT SHOULD BETRAY HIM, BEING ONE OF THE TWELVE....John 6:70-71 KJV.*

When Jesus needed to be tough, his words were quite direct, and often pretty harsh. He didn't beat around the bush, worrying about how to delicately approach the wicked. He wasn't concerned about bringing up the subject of their bad behavior in such a way that they wouldn't say he was "being mean," their feelings wouldn't be hurt, and they wouldn't be insulted. However, his firm rebukes and stern reprimands did not mean that he didn't love those he chastised. Loving and rebuke are not mutually exclusive. Listen to the Lord's rebuke of his beloved apostle Simon Peter:

BUT HE TURNED, AND SAID UNTO PETER, GET THEE BEHIND ME, SATAN: THOU ART AN OFFENCE UNTO

ME: FOR THOU SAVOUREST NOT THE THINGS THAT BE OF GOD, BUT THOSE THAT BE OF MEN....Matthew 16:23 KJV.

So we see, by Jesus' example, that we can love someone, and still confront them on it when they do wrong.

Do these words sound like they come from an endlessly patient and tolerant Jesus?:

"YOU SNAKES! YOU BROOD OF VIPERS! HOW WILL YOU ESCAPE BEING CONDEMNED TO HELL?"...Matthew 23:33NIV.

O GENERATION OF VIPERS, HOW CAN YE, BEING EVIL, SPEAK GOOD THINGS? FOR OUT OF THE ABUNDANCE OF THE HEART THE MOUTH SPEAKETH. A GOOD MAN OUT OF THE GOOD TREASURE OF THE HEART BRINGETH FORTH GOOD THINGS: AND AN EVIL MAN OUT OF THE EVIL TREASURE BRINGETH FORTH EVIL THINGS. BUT I SAY UNTO YOU, THAT EVERY IDLE WORD THAT MEN SHALL SPEAK, THEY SHALL GIVE ACCOUNT THEREOF IN THE DAY OF JUDGMENT. FOR BY THY WORDS THOU SHALT BE JUSTIFIED, AND BY THY WORDS THOU SHALT BE CONDEMNED...Matthew 12:34-37 KJV.

I don't know about you, but Jesus' words sound pretty tough to me. Some of his strongest rebukes were recorded in the Seven Woes of the Pharisees. A few examples are:

WOE TO YOU, TEACHERS OF THE LAW AND PHARISEES, YOU HYPOCRITES! YOU SHUT THE KINGDOM OF HEAVEN IN MEN'S FACES. YOU YOURSELVES DO NOT ENTER, NOR WILL YOU LET THOSE ENTER WHO ARE

TRYING TO. WOE TO YOU, TEACHERS OF THE LAW AND PHARISEES, YOU HYPOCRITES! YOU TRAVEL OVER LAND AND SEA TO WIN A SINGLE CONVERT, AND WHEN HE BECOMES ONE, YOU MAKE HIM TWICE AS MUCH A SON OF HELL AS YOU ARE....Matthew 23:13-15 NIV.

WOE TO YOU, SCRIBES AND PHARISEES, HYPOCRITES! FOR YOU PAY TITHE OF MINT AND ANISE AND CUMMIN, AND HAVE NEGLECTED THE WEIGHTIER MATTERS OF THE LAW: JUSTICE AND MERCY AND FAITH. THESE YOU OUGHT TO HAVE DONE, WITHOUT LEAVING THE OTHERS UNDONE. BLIND GUIDES, WHO STRAIN OUT A GNAT AND SWALLOW A CAMEL! WOE TO YOU, SCRIBES AND PHARISEES, HYPOCRITES! FOR YOU CLEANSE THE OUTSIDE OF THE CUP AND DISH, BUT INSIDE THEY ARE FULL OF EXTORTION AND SELF-INDULGENCE. BLIND PHARISEE, FIRST CLEANSE THE INSIDE OF THE CUP AND DISH, THAT THE OUTSIDE OF THEM MAY BE CLEAN ALSO. WOE TO YOU, SCRIBES AND PHARISEES, HYPOCRITES! FOR YOU ARE LIKE WHITEWASHED TOMBS WHICH INDEED APPEAR BEAUTIFUL OUTWARDLY, BUT INSIDE ARE FULL OF DEAD MEN'S BONES AND ALL UNCLEANNESS. EVEN SO YOU ALSO OUTWARDLY APPEAR RIGHTEOUS TO MEN, BUT INSIDE YOU ARE FULL OF HYPOCRISY AND LAWLESSNESS.....Matthew 23:23-28 NKJV.

When we think of Jesus being falsely accused and persecuted by the Jews, interrogated by Pilate, tortured and humiliated by the Roman soldiers, and finally dragged off and crucified, it certainly seems as though his patience with these people was endless. After all, he is God. Why didn't he stop them? When we consider this situation, Jesus does indeed seem to be a passive, meek person who would put up with just about anything. He could have struck them all dead in the blink of an eye; but instead, he just suffered through their abuse. Jesus seemed passive and patient then, because he was intentionally acting passive and patient! He allowed himself to be abused and killed in order to fulfill the prophecies in the scriptures, so that we might be saved by his precious blood. Those who persecuted and murdered him were just pawns in the drama that needed to be played out so that we could believe that Jesus was the Son of God. Their abuse served his purpose, and so he permitted it:

LET NOT YOUR HEART BE TROUBLED: YE BELIEVE IN GOD, BELIEVE ALSO IN ME. IN MY FATHER'S HOUSE ARE MANY MANSIONS: IF IT WERE NOT SO, I WOULD HAVE TOLD YOU. I GO TO PREPARE A PLACE FOR YOU. AND IF I GO AND PREPARE A PLACE FOR YOU, I WILL COME AGAIN, AND RECEIVE YOU UNTO MYSELF; THAT WHERE I AM, THERE YE MAY BE ALSO….John 14:1-3 KJV.

YET A LITTLE WHILE, AND THE WORLD SEETH ME NO MORE; BUT YE SEE ME: BECAUSE I LIVE, YE SHALL LIVE ALSO…John 14:19 KJV.

IF YOU LOVED ME, YOU WOULD REJOICE BECAUSE I SAID, "I AM GOING TO THE FATHER," FOR MY FATHER IS GREATER THAN I. AND NOW I HAVE TOLD YOU BEFORE IT COMES, THAT WHEN IT DOES COME TO PASS, YOU MAY BELIEVE. I WILL NO LONGER TALK MUCH WITH YOU, FOR THE RULER OF THIS WORLD IS COMING, AND HE HAS NOTHING IN ME. BUT THAT THE WORLD MAY KNOW THAT I LOVE THE FATHER, AND AS THE FATHER GAVE ME COMMANDMENT, SO I DO. ARISE, LET US GO FROM HERE….John 14:28-31 NKJV.

And so we see that Jesus did not just meekly allow himself to be tortured and killed. To believe that would be the same as believing that our Savior was weak and cowardly. On the contrary, the torture and death of Jesus proved that he was incredibly strong and courageous. Although he knew what was to come, and desired to be spared such horrible suffering if there was any other way, he also knew what he had to do to save us, and he did it. He loved us so much that he laid down his life for us, knowing how much pain and suffering he would have to endure. This was not a passive man who refused to put up a fight. This is someone who was tough as nails. His murder *was* his fight, the fight he was destined for, the fight for our salvation, and he did not back down from it. Before the fall of man, the wheels had been set in motion for the ultimate showdown between good and evil, between Jesus and Satan, which we learn about in the Book of Revelation. Without the crucifixion and resurrection of Jesus, the rest of the prophecies could not be fulfilled. We would not be spending eternity in the presence of our glorious Lord, and the final triumph of God over Satan, good over evil, would never happen.

It was Jesus' destiny to fight evil on a cosmic level, so far beyond our understanding that we can hardly begin to fathom it. This is what the Book of Revelation speaks of. Our fight against evil is the tiniest of specks in God's grand plan. But fight against it we must, because that *is* what Jesus would do, and that is what he *did* do. You see, we are all given our battle, just like Jesus was. During his time on earth, Jesus was given many "minor" battles to fight, and so are we. Then he was given a "major" one, and most of us will face that as well. He has not yet fought his final fight, and neither have most of us- but one day we all will. And then we will put on the full armor of God (Ephesians 6:10-19) and go to battle again.

So, when faced with abuse, cruelty, unlovingness, hurtfulness, evil and wickedness, let's ask ourselves, WWJRD? What Would

Jesus *REALLY* Do? And then pray for the wisdom and courage to stand up against evil in all its forms.

> *I HAVE FOUGHT A GOOD FIGHT, I HAVE FINISHED MY COURSE, I HAVE KEPT THE FAITH: HENCEFORTH THERE IS LAID UP FOR ME A CROWN OF RIGHTEOUSNESS, WHICH THE LORD, THE RIGHTEOUS JUDGE, SHALL GIVE ME AT THAT DAY: AND NOT TO ME ONLY, BUT UNTO ALL THEM ALSO THAT LOVE HIS APPEARING....2 Timothy 4:7-8 KJV.*

Epilogue: God is Not an Abuse-Enabler

Whenever I get an email calling me and the people who comment on my social media pages "bad Christians" because of what we teach, I always think how amazing it is that even educated people don't realize how much of themselves they give away by their comments. It's so easy for those of us with experience and Holy Ghost-given discernment to tell if they are 1) a narcissist, psychopath or sociopath, 2) a disgruntled no-contact parent, relative or friend blaming everybody else but themselves for encouraging their victim to dump them, 3) a psychologist or therapist who feels bad for the abusers because she was taught that every behavior is an "illness" and can't be helped, rather than a choice, 4) a Jezebel spirit trying to win people over to her point of view and get attention for herself, 5) an abuser who is enraged over being challenged and exposed, 6) a demon-infested abuse-enabler who is trying to get us to stop doing God's work and making his father, the devil, mad, 7) or a baby, milk-fed, "feel good" Christian who has not studied the Bible in depth and been given understanding from the Holy Ghost, and who for some insane reason believes that God *wants us* to tolerate, overlook, cover up and even lie about evil, and just turn a blind eye when someone is being abused.

When those Holier-Than-Thous teach this nonsense, they are teaching people that God is an abuse-enabler, and driving his children away from him. They are lying about God, they are slandering God, they are turning the naïve and innocent away from God and hindering them from feeling his love. And amazingly, they still boast that *they* are the "good" Christians, and we are the "bad," for holding the wicked accountable for their behavior. Oh, pull-eeze.

Real Christians follow the Bible, and the Bible is not "feel-good Christianity." God does not teach tolerance of evil. God does not teach unconditional forgiveness; he teaches repentance first.

He calls us to speak the truth, not hide it, and to confront evil, not overlook it. He tells us to expose evil, not cover it up. God calls people who do what abusers do "wicked," and he commands us, repeatedly, to shun the wicked. Not to take revenge, because vengeance is his, but to stay away and not contaminate ourselves. Staying away from the wicked is not "revenge."

If we follow God's biblical teachings for dealing with the evil, some people might even see the error of their ways, turn to God, repent and be saved. It might take rebuke, the withholding of forgiveness until it is merited, and/or shunning, to accomplish this, because ungodly people are usually more influenced by social censure and pressure than by the ideas of doing the right thing or pleasing the Lord. By trying to bully us into ignoring and overlooking the wickedness of abusers, holier-than-thou abuse-defenders are preventing a chance at their salvation, and therefore doing the devil's work.

When an abuse-enabler chastises us with platitudes like "God wants us to love our abusers," he reveals his lack of critical thinking skills and logic, because one thing has nothing to do with the other. Who says we don't love them? When abuse-enablers slander the righteous of God, *whose true spirit they don't even know*, or put words in their mouths, they sound like fools. It's ridiculous to think you can tell other adults, especially those you don't know extremely well, what they must be thinking or feeling, or what their "real motivations" must be. Holier-Than-Thous seem to have a mental "disconnect"-an inability to think about what they say and if it's really connected and relevant, or just plain stupid, illogical, and based on assumptions they have no way of knowing. They have no way of knowing whether or not someone loves someone else, they cannot see into our hearts and minds. They are spiritually blinded, ignorant, and unqualified to judge the saints.

People who criticize God's children for taking a stand against evil instead of "overlooking" or "tolerating" it, are revealing their own biblical ignorance by stating that these things are not "Christian" or "biblical" or "what God wants." They are W.r.o.n.g. Everything we teach is in the Bible. The fact that they haven't found it yet doesn't mean it's not there. They need to not just read, but study, and ask the Holy Ghost for understanding. They could try actually looking up the chapters and verses that we quote. That is, if they even own a Bible.

It makes absolutely no sense to chastise abuse victims and defend abusers. Normal people do not do this. This shows that you have issues of your own going on. The fact that abusers and the Flying Monkeys who defend them consider merely speaking the truth and staying away "taking revenge" is not our problem. It is their typical drama and exaggerated response habit surfacing. Narcissists and psychopaths like to pretend that *any* complaint, exposure, protest or consequence of their own behavior is the victim being "bad" in some way, but that is simply not true.

I sometimes have to remind Monkeys that I am not here to help abusers. My mission is to help survivors heal. That's what the Lord has ordained me to do. How anyone could possibly have a problem with that is just plain demented, but I get complaints from the children of the devil on a regular basis. They just don't see how crazy and evil they sound.

Here's the thing about so-called "personality-disordered" abusers. It is up to them to make better choices, get treatment or whatever. When you start hurting other people, you have crossed the line. You can claim to have whatever issues you like, but you have no right to inflict your issues on anybody else. Control yourself, or lock yourself in the house and stay out of civilized society so you can avoid temptation and in so doing, avoid sinning. Turn to God and save your soul. Again, I am not here to help abusers, but if you are an abuser, I just gave you a helpful piece of advice. Resist the devil and he will flee from you (James 4:7). He can only tempt you, but nobody can *make* you abuse someone else. You choose to abuse.

When anyone objects to teaching what the Bible says about rebuking, repentance, the granting or withholding forgiveness, and shunning the wicked, they are showing the whole world exactly what they are, what *their* mental and spiritual state is, and whose side they are on- Satan's or God's.

Meanwhile, whenever Satan tries to confuse the issue, all we have to remember is that God is not an abuse-enabler. He never said anything, and the Bible never says anything, that would facilitate abuse or make it easier for the wicked to continue in their sin. Anyone who claims otherwise is not speaking for God.

May God bless you abundantly as you seek his truths and fight the good fight.

LET NO ONE DECEIVE YOU WITH EMPTY WORDS, FOR BECAUSE OF THESE THINGS THE WRATH OF GOD COMES UPON THE SONS OF DISOBEDIENCE. THEREFORE DO NOT BE PARTAKERS WITH THEM. FOR YOU WERE ONCE DARKNESS, BUT NOW YOU ARE LIGHT IN THE LORD. WALK AS CHILDREN OF LIGHT (FOR THE FRUIT OF THE SPIRIT IS IN ALL GOODNESS, RIGHTEOUSNESS, AND TRUTH), FINDING OUT WHAT IS ACCEPTABLE TO THE LORD. AND HAVE NO FELLOWSHIP WITH THE UNFRUITFUL WORKS OF DARKNESS, BUT RATHER EXPOSE THEM....Ephesians 5:6-11 NKJV.

Also by Sister Renee Pittelli

The Christian's Guide to No Contact
Breaking the Bonds of Adult Child Abuse
Narcissistic Predicaments
Narcissistic Confrontations
The Family Freeloader

Made in the USA
San Bernardino, CA
09 February 2018